SPIDERS

PHOTOGUIDE

Text by Paul Hillyard
The Natural History Museum,
London

Photographic Consultants
Premaphotos Wildlife

HarperCollins*Publishers*

HarperCollins*Publishers*
PO Box, Glasgow G4 0NB
First published 1997

Reprint 9 8 7 6 5 4 3 2 1

ISBN 0 00 470904 7

Typeset by TJ Graphics

Printed in Italy by Amadeus S.p.A.

CONTENTS KEY

The 200 spiders in this book have been selected from the world's 35,000 known species for their special interest, appearance or abundance. Each species is described and illustrated together with its Latin and English names, and species that are particulary venomous are indicated by a skull and crossbones. The world's 105 families of spiders, each containing closely related species, are sorted in this book into eight groups comprised of one or a number of similar families. The ninth group includes some relatives of spiders. These nine groups are characterised by a small symbol at the top of the page, as follows:

Primitive Spiders (pp. 20–39)
Mostly large or very large spiders, this group of more than a dozen families includes the tarantulas (family Theraphosidae), trap-door spiders (e.g. Ctenizidae), purse-web spiders (Atypidae) and some funnel-web spiders (e.g. Dipluridae).

Six-eyed Spiders (pp. 40–54)
A convenient grouping of fewer than 10 families of small to medium-sized spiders including the spitting spiders (Scytodidae), recluse spiders (Loxoscelidae), tube-web weavers (Segestridae) and daddy-longlegs spiders (Pholcidae; some have eight eyes).

Lace-web Weavers (pp. 55–70)
Also known as the cribellates, these mostly small to medium-sized spiders form a group of more than a dozen families including Dictynidae, Eresidae, Amaurobiidae, Deinopidae and Uloboridae.

Tangle- & Sheet-web Weavers (pp. 71–96)
Tangle-web weavers belong to a single, large family (Theridiidae) of small to medium-sized spiders often with round abdomens. The sheet-web weavers are a group of about a dozen families ranging in size from the tiny Linyphiidae to the medium-sized Agelenidae.

Orb-weavers (pp. 97–156)
The main families of orb-weavers are the Araneidae, Tetragnathidae and Metidae. In most cases the males are smaller than the females; in some, e.g. spiny-backed spiders and golden-orb weavers, the males are very much smaller.

Hunting Spiders (pp. 157–202)
Hunting spiders belong to a large number of families of small to large spiders including the wolf spiders (Lycosidae), wandering spiders (Ctenidae), nursery-web spiders (Pisauridae), huntsman spiders (Heteropodidae) and lynx spiders (Oxyopidae).

Crab Spiders (pp. 203–219)
The two main kinds of these small to medium-sized spiders are the slow-moving species in the family Thomisidae and the more active species in the family Philodromidae.

Jumping Spiders (pp. 220–239)
The large number of jumping spiders worldwide (about 4000 species) belongs to a single family, the Salticidae. Jumping spiders are mostly small – up to 20 mm body length.

Relatives of Spiders (pp. 240–247)

Introduction

Spiders are among the stars of the natural world and the variety of species is amazing. They occur virtually everywhere and are one of the most successful groups of animals. Their success is based on their venom, which is used for attack and defence (see p. 16), and on the many uses they have for silk, which is employed with great skill and ingenuity (see p. 10).

The number of known species of spiders in the world is about 35,000. However, it is estimated that a further 35,000 remain to be discovered, thus the true number in existence may be 70,000. In this book, the species that have been selected are those that are likely to be noticed because they are common or have a striking appearance.

The largest of all spiders is the Goliath Tarantula of South America (p.29); it has a leg span of 25 cm. The smallest fully-grown spider, the male of a species called *Patu digua*, has a body length of just 0.37 mm, which is smaller than a pin-head. (Sizes given for the species in this book refer to body length, not leg span.) Apart from size, spiders also vary greatly in their appearance. While some are brightly coloured, others are very inconspicuous. Some are fat-bodied, others resemble worms, and many are bizarrely decorated with strange surface features.

Spiders avoid danger in a number of ways. Many have impenetrable hiding places, and others use colour for concealment; for example, green spiders live among leaves, while red, yellow and white ones live among flowers. Some are beautifully camouflaged against backgrounds such as sand or lichen, or they resemble a twig, and others go unrecognised because they mimic ants – insects which

5

many predators leave alone.

With notable exceptions, most spiders have poor eyesight, but they are highly sensitive to vibrations, especially from insects. Web-building spiders detect vibrations transmitted to them via the web's silk threads. Hunting spiders, which do not build webs, detect vibrations across the ground and air. Aquatic spiders radiate their legs in all directions on the water's surface to pick up vibrations.

SPIDERS AND THEIR RELATIVES

Spiders are related to scorpions, pseudoscorpions, whip scorpions (or vinegaroons), whip spiders, camel spiders, ricinuleids, harvestmen, mites and ticks. All these eight-legged creatures are classified as arachnids. Spiders form an order which is distinguished from the other arachnid orders by: a body in two parts connected by a narrow waist; male sex organs on the ends of the palps (feelers); spinnerets for silk production, and the absence of a tail. Generally, arachnids are predators but the ticks and some mites are parasites.

There are three groups (suborders) of spiders: (1) the rare liphistiomorphs ('fossil' trap-door spiders); (2) the mygalomorphs (trap-door spiders, purse-web spiders and tarantulas); and (3) the araneomorphs, or 'true' spiders, which are the typical and most numerous kinds. Because of their diversity, spiders are classified into more than 100 families. In this book, spiders included in the first category are primitive spiders from the first two suborders. The liphistiomorphs and mygalomorphs are considered 'primitive' because of the way their jaws work (see diagram, p. 16) and because they have only book lungs for breathing

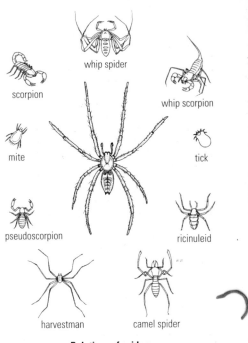

whip spider

scorpion

whip scorpion

mite

tick

pseudoscorpion

ricinuleid

harvestman

camel spider

Relatives of spiders

and lack a system of fine tubes (tracheae). The other seven categories in the book are araneomorphs or 'true' spiders.

ANATOMY

A spider is an arthropod, which means that the legs are jointed and the body has a rigid outer skeleton (**exoskeleton**). Spiders differ from other arthropods, such as insects, in having eight legs and a body in two parts.

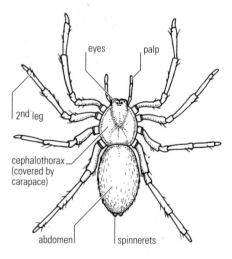

View of spider from above

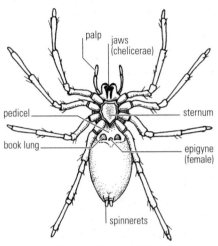

View of spider from below

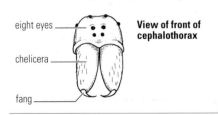

View of front of cephalothorax

9

Furthermore, spiders lack antennae and never possess wings, which are usually present in insects. The jaws of spiders function by stabbing (to inject venom) and the food is digested externally and sucked in as a liquid.

The front half of the body, the combined head and thorax (**cephalothorax**), carries the jaws (**chelicerae**), eyes, eight legs and two **palps** (feelers). It contains the brain and is protected by a hard cover (**carapace**). Most spiders have eight eyes but some have only six or fewer. The jointed legs are made up of seven segments. Adult male spiders have a pair of sex organs on the ends of their palps.

The rear half of the body, the **abdomen**, is connected to the front half by a narrow waist (**pedicel**). Being soft, the abdomen is expandable when fully fed or swollen with eggs. The abdomen contains the heart, digestive tract, reproductive organs, respiratory openings and silk glands. Silk emerges from the **spinnerets** at the end of the abdomen. The female reproductive opening (**epigyne**) is located on the underside of the abdomen.

PRODUCTION AND USES OF SILK

Spider silk is a remarkable material which, though extremely fine, is very strong, light and elastic. It comes from glands in the abdomen and is drawn out rather than squeezed out. The drawing process (pulled by a leg, for example) converts it from a liquid to a solid. Up to six different glands produce silk of different types for various uses. One gland found in orb-weavers makes gummy silk to make webs sticky.

There are many different kinds of webs. They range in complexity from single threads to orb-webs with hundreds

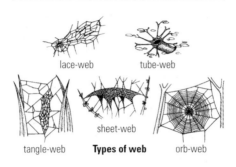

lace-web

tube-web

tangle-web

sheet-web

Types of web

orb-web

Uses of silk

trap-door

egg sac

spider emitting gossamer
prior to becoming airborne

spider descending
on dragline

of connections. Other types include the sheet-webs, lace-webs, tangle-webs, purse-webs and tube-webs. Often the species of spider can be recognised by the details of a web, without seeing its weaver.

All spiders make silk but only about half of them actually build webs to catch insects. The other half make no webs but catch their prey with tactics ranging from running to stalking, leaping and ambushing. Besides making webs, silk is used for constructing trap-doors and nests (**retreats** and **sacs**), egg cocoons, and for wrapping prey (**swathing band**). Also, spiders trail a line of silk (**dragline**) which acts as a safety line and can be climbed later if the spider drops down. Many small and young spiders make long lines of silk (**gossamer**) for their dispersal by air (**ballooning**).

GROWTH

Spiders and other arthropods have a rigid skeleton on the outside of the body (exoskeleton). In order to grow, the old exoskeleton is shed, or moulted, leaving a soft outer covering which expands until it hardens. The moults number five or fewer in small species, while larger, more long-lived species require up to double this number. An old skin (**exuvium**) can be mistaken for the real corpse of a spider.

Spiders preparing to moult lose interest in eating for many days. Some species seal themselves into a moulting chamber while others simply hang from a line in their web. First, the carapace lifts like a lid and then the sides of the abdomen split. Extracting the legs and palps is the trickiest part. If a leg remains stuck, it can be broken off, and lost legs or palps may be regenerated during the next moult. Spiders frequently die while moulting.

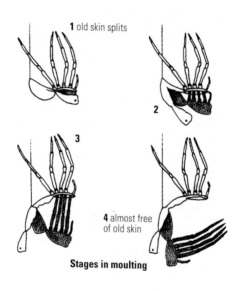

1 old skin splits

2

3

4 almost free of old skin

Stages in moulting

When the body is free, it hangs from a thread and expands to its new size; also the relative proportions of the body change. The carapace becomes larger while the abdomen is temporarily smaller. At the final moult, the sex organs become fully developed: the external organs of the male become visible on the ends of the palps, and those of the female on the underside of the abdomen.

COURTSHIP & REPRODUCTION

The courtship rituals of spiders include some of the most remarkable behaviour in the Animal Kingdom. A male needs to communicate to the (usually) larger female to prevent her confusing him with prey and so eating him. Males of different species have their own unique repertoire of signals. Web-spinning species introduce themselves by plucking and vibrating the web's threads. Male hunting spiders, such as wolf spiders and jumping spiders, have good eyesight and make visual signals by dancing and waving their strikingly-marked legs and palps. One particular species seduces the female with an offering of food.

Spiders have an unusual method of reproduction. Before courtship, the male fills his syringe-like palps with a drop of sperm from an opening on the underside of the body. During mating, one palp at a time is inserted into the female and rhythmically squeezed to transfer the sperm. The male palp and female epigyne of each species fit together like a lock and key.

Depending on the species, spiders lay from one to over 1000 eggs per batch. In most species the female encloses her batch of eggs in a protective silk sac. Egg sacs may be hidden in crevices or among leaves. Some mother spiders never again see their eggs but others guard them and some carry their eggs around with them, usually attached to the jaws or to the spinnerets.

When the eggs hatch, the 'spiderlings' look like miniatures of their parents. Most are able to look after themselves, but the young of some species, for example the Nursery Web Spider, are cared for by their mothers.

Courtship of orb-weavers

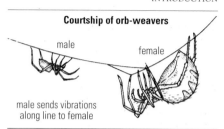

male   female

male sends vibrations
along line to female

Courtship of jumping spiders

male signals with legs and palps to female

View of male palp

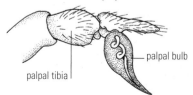

palpal bulb

palpal tibia

SPIDER VENOM, BITES & TREATMENT

A few notorious species of spiders in the world (marked 🕷 and 🕷 🕷 in this book) are venomous to humans, but the majority may be considered harmless. However, many spiders will give a nip if handled roughly. With the exception of one family of spiders (Uloboridae), all produce venom, but this is intended to deal with insects and its effect on humans is usually only slight. The venom is

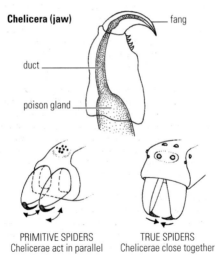

Chelicera (jaw)

fang

duct

poison gland

PRIMITIVE SPIDERS
Chelicerae act in parallel

TRUE SPIDERS
Chelicerae close together

produced in a gland at the base of each of the two chelicerae (jaws). When the spider bites, venom passes along ducts in the chelicerae and is ejected from openings at the end of the fangs (the moving part of the chelicerae).

The spiders whose venom causes relatively serious effects may be divided into two categories: neurotoxic and cytotoxic. Black Widow spiders and Sydney Funnel-web spiders are examples of species that have venoms with a neurotoxic effect, i.e. the victim's nervous system is affected. Usually, the nerve/muscle junctions are inhibited, causing paralysis. If death results it is likely to ensue from paralysis of the respiratory system. By contrast, Recluse spiders (*Loxosceles* spp.) are examples of species that produce a cytotoxic effect, i.e. tissue is damaged, particularly around the site of the bite.

Some of the notorious spiders that used to cause death in parts of the world, years ago, no longer do so because of the development of specific anti-venoms. However, where specific anti-venom is not available, the best general treatment for a spider bite is an intravenous dose of calcium gluconate. Unfortunately, spiders often get the blame for bites from many other creatures. The sign of a spider bite is a double puncture-mark but, to be on the safe side, it is advisable to check with a doctor.

WHERE TO FIND SPIDERS

There are few places on Earth without spiders. They live in all sorts of habitats ranging from rainforests to deserts, from mountain tops to caves and, as is well known, spiders have a great affinity for buildings. Some specialised species live on or in the water, both fresh and salt. The ice cap of

Antarctica is perhaps the only part of the world that has no spiders.

The richest habitats for spiders are forests and flowery meadows; probably the greatest diversity of species is found in the tropical rainforests. The number of individuals living in undisturbed English meadows has been estimated at more than five million spiders per hectare during the month of October.

It is easy to observe spiders, especially in the autumn when their webs festoon bushes and grass. Many spiders like dark, sheltered places, so turning over stones or rubbish usually reveals plenty. Remember also that they come in many different sizes so be prepared for tiny as well as large ones.

One of the great advantages of studying spiders is that there are always some to be found, no matter what the time of year. However, certain seasons are better than others. In temperate countries, the life cycle of most species occupies a full year, but part of the year is spent in the egg stage, another part is spent as a growing juvenile, and the remaining part is spent as an adult. In this book, the notes on season for each species indicate the months when the adults are present and active. These periods are approximate and may vary from region to region.

Spiders usually mature at times of the year when insect abundance, and their own activity, is high or about to become high. In tropical localities with plenty of insects, seasonality may not be easy to define, as some species may have more than one generation in a year. By contrast, in the Arctic, the season of spider activity usually coincides with the short summer. In the case of spiders that live for a number of years, for example tarantulas, the adults are present throughout the year, but their periods of activity may be determined by the onset of seasonal rains.

HOW TO KEEP SPIDERS

The easiest spiders to look after are the *Tegenaria* house spiders. These may be found in outbuildings such as sheds and garages and they adapt readily to a handy container in which they can build a sheet web. In general, spiders need to be given some drops of water. For food, they should be offered insects of a size similar to themselves. These may be household insects or cultivated insects such as mealworm beetles which are obtainable from pet shops. Larger spiders and tarantulas should be fed on crickets or cockroaches. For very small and young spiders, fruit flies are most suitable. Using rotten fruit, it is possible to attract fruit flies and then maintain them as a breeding culture.

Typically, spiders live for a year or two, though some tarantulas have lived for as long as 30 years in captivity. Because they have the ability to retain sperm over very long periods, female spiders often produce an egg cocoon after feeding. Observing the life-cycles of spiders and comparing the different species makes a very interesting hobby. It can be especially satisfying to discover that your orb-weaver has spun a fresh orb-web!

PHOTOGRAPHS

Each species described in this book is illustrated with a full colour photograph. In species where the male and female differ in appearance, the female is illustrated unless otherwise stated.

19

PRIMITIVE SPIDERS

Primitive spiders have jaws resembling a pair of pick-axes (see p. 16) and they need to rise up on their back legs in order to strike. Most of them are large, and males are usually not much smaller than females. They also have two pairs of book lungs and lack the network of fine breathing tubes (tracheae) of other spiders. Usually, the eight tiny eyes form a close group.

Primitive spiders (approximately 15 families) belong to the suborders Liphistiomorphae ('fossil' trap-door spiders) and Mygalomorphae (e.g. tarantulas, trap-door spiders, purse-web spiders and funnel-web spiders of Australia). All other 'true' or typical spiders are placed in the third and largest suborder, the Araneomorphae.

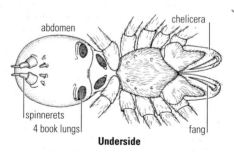

Underside

GIANT TRAP-DOOR SPIDER *Liphistius desultor*

An impressive, bluish-grey spider with an orange carapace and blue and orange legs. It lives in a silk-lined burrow and emerges to catch passing insects. On the ground, the trap-door is very difficult to find because it is extremely well camouflaged. *Liphistius* is virtually a 'living fossil' – the bands across the abdomen are remnants of primitive body divisions that have entirely disappeared in other spiders. There are 20 or so known species of *Liphistius* in SE Asia.

Size	Female to 40 mm; male to 30 mm.
Web	8 signal lines radiate from a hinged trap-door.
Habitat	Sloping banks in forest and alongside roads.
Range	Penang and other localities in W Malaysia.
Season	Adult females all year; males February–August.

21

PURSE-WEB SPIDER *Atypus affinis*

An unusual species that lives inside a strange web resembling the finger of a glove. The spider's carapace and legs are glossy olive-grey and the abdomen is reddish-brown. The jaws are huge but the legs are short. Unsuspecting flies and other insects that alight on the web are bitten through the webbing and dragged inside by the spider. After the uneaten remains of the prey are thrown out, the hole in the web is repaired.

Size Female to 16 mm; male to 12 mm.
Web Deep, silk-lined burrow emerging above ground as a camouflaged tube (the 'purse-web').
Habitat Grass and shrubs, in sandy or chalky areas.
Range Europe, N Africa and W Asia.
Season Adult females all year; males in late summer.

MOGGRIDGE'S TRAP-DOOR SPIDER *Cteniza moggridgei*

Difficult to find because it lives in a burrow and emerges only very briefly to intercept its prey. Above ground all that can be seen is a well-fitting trap-door made of silk and soil. The door keeps out water and predators but at night it is opened halfway. The female is sturdy with large jaws; she has a dark, glossy carapace, a beige or grey abdomen and short, stout legs. The smaller male is slimmer.

Size	Female to 18 mm; male to 13 mm.
Web	None, but the burrow is silk-lined.
Habitat	Hillsides and banks of earth suitable for burrowing.
Range	S France, Corsica and Italy.
Season	Adult females all year; males active in autumn.

Greek Trap-door Spider *Cyrtocarenum* sp.

Another spider that lives in a secret burrow, dug using a spiny rake on the front of the jaws. The thick, cork-like door is held shut by the spider which emerges only briefly to catch its prey, usually ants or beetles. The sturdy female has large jaws, a glossy, dark brown, raised carapace, a yellow-grey abdomen and short, stout legs. The smaller, slimmer male has a dark carapace and pale abdomen.

Size Female to 32 mm; male to 24 mm.
Web None, but the burrow is silk-lined.
Habitat Sunny hillsides with soil suitable for digging burrows.
Range Greece.
Season Adult females all year; males during warm, rainy seasons.

AUSTRALIAN TRAP-DOOR SPIDER *Aname sp.*

A species that lives in a burrow without a door. The female has a pale brown abdomen and a low, reddish-brown carapace with eyes on a tubercle which is about twice as wide as long. The male (shown here) is similar but slimmer. During the season when wandering in search of a female, he runs rapidly and is aggressive if provoked. When mating, the spurs on the male's first legs lock the female's jaws out of harm's way.

Size Female to 30 mm; male to 24 mm.
Web None, but the burrow is silk-lined.
Habitat Open ground with soil suitable for burrowing.
Range Western Australia.
Season Adult females probably all year; males August–December.

25

SYDNEY FUNNEL-WEB SPIDER *Atrax robustus*

One of the deadliest spiders in the world. The aggressive male causes most of the bites. Both male and female are bluish-black with two long spinnerets at the end of the abdomen. The male's second pair of legs has spurs to restrain the female during mating. At night the spider moves to one of the web's entrances where it snatches insects, snails and small vertebrates.

Size Female to 35 mm; male to 25 mm.
Web A funnel-web; usually issues from a burrow and has trip-threads around the entrance(s).
Habitat Forest edges and gardens.
Range Australia: New South Wales and Victoria .
Season Adult females all year; males active November–March.

SPANISH FUNNEL-WEB SPIDER *Macrothele calpeiana*

One of the largest and most fierce-looking spiders in Europe. As most of its relatives live in the tropics, this is a unique species which deserves special appreciation. The satin-black colour and the long flexible spinnerets are unmistakable. The carapace is low and flat and the eyes are in a compact group. The female resembles the male but has a larger abdomen.

Size Female to 32 mm; male to 22 mm.
Web A funnel-web with trip-threads around the entrance, built among stones or roots.
Habitat Pine or cork oak forests; also roadsides.
Range W Andalucia (Spain) and NW Africa.
Season Adult females all year; males active March–October.

27

PINK-TOED TARANTULA _Avicularia avicularia_

The first 'tarantula' to be described (by Linnaeus in 1758), and well known because of its orange or pink 'toes' and relatively wide range. The sooty-black carapace and abdomen are clothed in long hairs. This spider builds a silken nest in folded banana leaves, for example, or within a pineapple plant. It may occasionally catch roosting birds, but the diet is mostly tree frogs and insects.

Size   Female to 50 mm; male to 35 mm.
Web   A tubular web extending from a hole.
Habitat   Trees and hollow stumps in plantations and humid forest.
Range   Guyana, Brazil, Venezuela and Trinidad.
Season   Adults probably all year; mating activity during rainy seasons.

GOLIATH TARANTULA *Theraphosa blondi*

This, the largest spider in the world, is powerful enough to feed on frogs, toads, lizards, mice and even small snakes. It is dark grey-brown, but the legs have masses of curly, reddish-brown hairs. The male's leg span reaches 25 cm. In both sexes the carapace is as wide as it is long. The female's abdomen is noticeably broad. By rubbing parts of the body, these spiders can make clearly audible sounds.

Size Female to 90 mm; male to 85 mm.
Web None, but lines of silk surround the burrow's entrance.
Habitat A deep burrow in tropical rainforest.
Range Venezuela, northern Brazil, Guyana, French Guiana and Suriname.
Season Adults likely to be present all year.

VIOLET-BLACK TARANTULA *Pamphobeteus sp.*

One of the large S American tarantulas. In the depths of the rainforest, a glimpse of this active and impressive spider is quite striking. The carapace and legs of the female are a velvety, slate-blue black and the abdomen is black with long brown hairs covering the rear half. The male is similar but the jaws, palps and legs show a violet sheen. The diet of this spider includes small reptiles.

Size	Female to 60 mm; male to 50 mm.
Web	None.
Habitat	Tropical rainforest.
Range	Peru and Bolivia (Amazonia).
Season	Adult females all year; male's season is uncertain.

TRINIDADIAN OLIVE TARANTULA *Hapalopus incei*

A modestly-sized, hairy tarantula. The carapace is dark brown with golden striae and the abdomen is grey-brown with a number of golden-olive bands. The species lives in holes in trees or makes a shallow burrow, sometimes in colonies. Mating is quite brief and the egg sac appears about one month later. After a further month's incubation, an average of 35 young spiders emerge.

Size	Female to 35 mm, male to 20 mm.
Web	Silk threads surround entrance to burrow.
Habitat	Tropical forest, scrub and roadsides.
Range	Trinidad.
Season	Adults probably all year; mating activity during rainy seasons.

MEXICAN RED-KNEE TARANTULA *Brachypelma smithi*

An exceptionally attractive species which has become a popular exotic pet. This tarantula is recognised by the orange or red knees. The abdomen varies from brown to black and the carapace is black with orange around the margin. The diet includes beetles, millipedes and lizards. These large spiders live for a number of years. Because of their popularity as pets, Mexican Red-knees need protection in their natural habitat.

Size   Female to 75 mm; male to 55 mm.
Web   None; excavates a deep burrow.
Habitat   Shady banks in forest and stony scrubland.
Range   Mexico: southern and western states.
Season   Adults all year; males visit females during rainy seasons.

ARIZONAN BLOND TARANTULA *Aphonopelma chalcodes*

A large pale spider which builds a burrow in desert country. The carapace of both male and female is clothed in short beige hairs and contrasts with the darker abdomen. At night the spider emerges to hunt prey, ranging from ants to small vertebrates, within a distance of three metres from the burrow. During the day the burrow's entrance is silked over. While mating, the spurs on the male's legs hold the female's fangs at bay.

Size Female to 60 mm; male to 45 mm.
Web None, but silk threads line a simple burrow.
Habitat Cactus desert and scrubland.
Range Arizona and northern Mexico.
Season Breeds in autumn, especially following rain; activity reduced in winter.

33

Sri Lankan Ornamental Tarantula *Poecilotheria fasciata*

A beautifully-marked but temperamental species. The dark abdomen has a broad, central, cream band edged in black, plus five oblique marks. The carapace is grey with cream markings. The legs are banded black and white, with yellow on the first two pairs. The male is relatively small and slender. These spiders are nocturnal and live in trees; their nest is usually built in a tree hole. Locally they are known as tree spiders.

Size	Female to 65 mm; male to 50 mm.
Web	A mass of silk surrounds the nest entrance.
Habitat	Tropical forest; sometimes in buildings.
Range	Sri Lanka.
Season	Adults all year; mating activity during hot, humid seasons.

VELVET TARANTULA *Lyrognathus robustus*

A handsome, burrowing tarantula. The carapace, abdomen and first half of the legs are dark brown with a blue iridescence (in certain angles of light). The second half of the legs are a paler brown, with some blue streaks. The last two pairs of legs are more hairy than the first two pairs. This spider emerges from its burrow in the evening to hunt on the floor of the rainforest.

Size	Female to 50 mm; male to 35 mm.
Web	None, but silk surrounds entrance to burrow.
Habitat	Tropical rainforest.
Range	W Malaysia.
Season	Adult females all year; males active during rainy seasons.

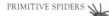

AUSTRALIAN WHISTLING TARANTULA *Selenocosmia* sp.

A brown tarantula with a dense covering of hairs and a pair of long spinnerets. It hunts insects and small vertebrates during the night but spends the day deep inside the burrow. When capturing prey and during courtship, it makes whistling sounds by rubbing the palps against the jaws. Aggressive if threatened, the venom is toxic to humans but not deadly.

Size Female to 55 mm; male to 40 mm.
Web The silk lining of the burrow opens to a funnel-shaped entrance.
Habitat Eucalypt forest, *Acacia* thickets and grassland.
Range Australia, including Queensland, Northern Territories and New South Wales.
Season Adults probably all year; mating activity during summer rains.

Horned Baboon Spider *Ceratogyrus darlingi*

A hairy, grey-brown tarantula with stout legs and a prominent, rear-facing horn in the middle of the carapace. Black lines radiate from the horn across the carapace. This spider lives in a deep, silk-lined burrow and emerges at night to hunt small vertebrates and insects. If provoked, it rears up with outstretched front legs and strikes downwards with the jaws. A wound may result but the venom is only mildly toxic to humans.

Size	Female to 65 mm; male to 45 mm.
Web	None, but silk threads extend from the burrow's entrance.
Habitat	Seasonal forest.
Range	E Africa: Zimbabwe and Mozambique.
Season	Adults all year; mating during rainy seasons.

COMMON BABOON SPIDER *Harpactira* sp.

A burrowing tarantula with a pair of long spinnerets. The female has a dark grey carapace, with pale striae, and a ginger-brown abdomen. The male is dark with reddish hairs on the abdomen. *Harpactira* is recognised by a transverse groove in the centre of the carapace. It usually excavates its holes but may use vacant animal burrows. It makes a buzzing sound by rubbing the palps against the jaws.

Size   Female to 50 mm; male to 40 mm.
Web   None, but rests during the day in a silk-lined retreat or burrow.
Habitat   *Acacia* scrub and grassland.
Range   Cape region of S Africa.
Season   Adults all year; mating activity during warm, humid seasons.

SIX-EYED SPIDERS

The six-eyed spiders are an assorted group of fewer than 10 families. These are small or medium-sized, mostly nocturnal spiders of various habits. Some spin webs but others have more unusual methods of catching prey. Under the microscope, their eye arrangements give a rather strange appearance.

Six-eyed spiders include the spitting spiders (Scytodidae), recluse spiders (Loxoscelidae) and tube-web spiders (Segestridae). The daddy-long-legs spiders (Pholcidae) are included in the group though some species have eight eyes. Most six-eyed web-spinners build rough webs but the tube-webs are recognised by the precise trip-lines which radiate from the opening.

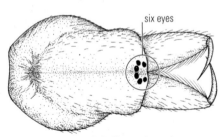

six eyes

Carapace and chelicerae from above

SIX-EYED CRAB SPIDER *Sicarius rugosus*

This species has a tough, leathery body and holds its legs out sideways like a crab. The flat carapace is broad and the eyes are in three pairs. It is a sluggish and secretive spider which often buries itself below the surface of the ground. *Sicarius* species are ancient spiders which existed before the separation of the African and S American continents over 100 million years ago.

Size	Female to 15 mm; male to 10 mm.
Web	None.
Habitat	Among sand, leaf litter and under rocks.
Range	Dry country in Central America.
Season	Adults all year; individuals probably live for a number of years.

SPITTING SPIDER *Scytodes thoracica*

A curious, slow-moving, nocturnal wanderer. It catches insects by squirting poisonous, gummy silk from the jaws. The gum is produced in enlarged venom glands inside a domed carapace. The eyes are in three pairs, the globular beige abdomen is spotted, and the legs are slender. The mother carries the ball of eggs in her jaws (shown here). Preying on clothes moths and other pests, these spiders should be welcomed in the home.

Size Female to 6 mm; male to 5 mm.
Web None, but retreats to a tangle of silk in a crevice.
Habitat Under stones, in caves, mines and buildings.
Range Cosmopolitan.
Season Adults all year.

ANDEAN SPITTING SPIDER *Scytodes globula*

A large spitting spider with long legs. Like the Spitting Spider (opposite), the carapace is highly domed to house the large venom glands which produce poisonous gum. The overall colour is beige with a strong dark brown pattern. At the front of the carapace, there is a pair of false 'eye' markings above the six true eyes. The mother spider carries the ball of about 50 eggs in her jaws, held together by a few silk threads (shown here).

Size	Female to 9 mm; male to 7 mm.
Web	None.
Habitat	Under stones, in caves and buildings.
Range	Chile and Argentina.
Season	Adults all year.

43

VIOLIN SPIDER *Loxosceles rufescens*

A delicate, beige-brown spider with long legs. It has a dark mark on the carapace resembling a violin. The eyes are arranged in three pairs. The abdomen is paler than the carapace. Violin Spiders generally roam at night in search of prey but they also weave a web to entangle insects. They are not aggressive and rarely bite humans. The eggs are laid in a loose sac in the web.

Size	Female to 8 mm; male to 7 mm.
Web	A rough sheet of sticky silk.
Habitat	Under stones and loose bark, in caves and buildings.
Range	S Europe and N Africa; introduced to Japan, N America, Australia and New Zealand.
Season	Adults all year.

BROWN RECLUSE SPIDER *Loxosceles reclusa*

A venomous but shy spider similar in appearance to the Violin Spider (opposite). In buildings, Brown Recluse Spiders are found in the corners of rooms, behind furniture and in cupboards. They spin an irregular web but also forage at night. During its nocturnal wandering, this spider may bite if it comes into contact with a human or gets caught up in clothing. A bite can cause an ulcer of the skin, and sometimes even death.

Size Female to 9 mm; male to 8 mm.
Web A rough sheet of sticky silk.
Habitat Under stones, rocks and loose tree bark; also in buildings.
Range S and central N America.
Season Adults all year.

45

DADDY-LONGLEGS SPIDER *Pholcus phalangioides*

A pale grey, delicate species with long, thin legs and an elongated body. Also called the Cellar Spider, it is associated with dark and damp places but is increasingly occupying ordinary rooms, where it eats household pests. It is a prolific breeder. When disturbed, the spider bounces up and down and becomes a blur. The mother carries the eggs, and babies when they hatch, in her mouthparts.

Size	Female to 10 mm; male to 10 mm (legs reach 40 mm).
Web	A flimsy cobweb, from which the spider hangs upside down.
Habitat	Caves and buildings, especially in cellars.
Range	Cosmopolitan.
Season	Adult females all year; males spring to autumn.

TROPICAL DADDY-LONGLEGS SPIDER *Smeringopus pallidus*

Similar to the Daddy-Longlegs Spider (opposite), this species has long, slender legs and a cylindrical abdomen. The abdomen is grey-brown with a pattern of pale streaks and the carapace is grey. The legs are dark with white rings near the joints; the legs detach easily. The web is vibrated to distract intruders. A ball of eggs is carried in the female's jaws (shown here). This household species has very small jaws and is totally harmless to humans.

Size Female to 8 mm; male to 6 mm.
Web An irregular, flimsy web.
Habitat Disused rooms, especially if dark and damp; also among rocks and under logs.
Range Pantropical.
Season Adults all year.

Short-bodied Cellar Spider _Physocyclus globosus_

This long-legged species has a short, grey abdomen which is spherical or sometimes triangular. The eyes (eight) are set close together on a dark mound; a dark band runs the length of the carapace. The spider runs very quickly across the web in response to vibrations from struggling insects, millipedes and other spiders. Prey is wrapped in swathing silk before being bitten. The mother carries the egg sac in her jaws.

Size Female to 5 mm; male to 4 mm.
Web A small untidy sheet from which the spider hangs upside down.
Habitat Caves and buildings (especially in cellars).
Range Cosmopolitan in warm countries.
Season Adults probably all year.

WINE CELLAR SPIDER *Psilochorus simoni*

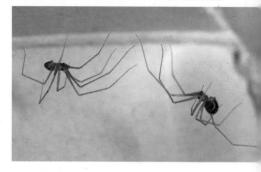

A small, long-legged species with a globular abdomen tinged blue or green. The spinnerets are underneath the abdomen instead of at the end. The pale carapace is circular and has a dark brown band which encloses the eyes and tapers to the rear. The legs are pale brown with dark and pale bands. Like others of its kind, this spider gyrates in its web when disturbed.

Size	Female to 3 mm; male to 2 mm.
Web	Made of loose, criss-cross threads, from which the spider hangs upside down.
Habitat	Buildings, especially in wine cellars.
Range	N America and Europe.
Season	Adults occur all year.

WOODLOUSE SPIDER *Dysdera crocata*

This species looks rather sinister with its large fangs, reddish carapace and legs contrasting with a cream or grey abdomen, and absence of hairs. The six eyes form a compact group. It usually lives close to numbers of woodlice, its favourite prey. It builds no snare but lives in a silk retreat, where the eggs are laid, and emerges at night on hunting excursions. The bite can be painful.

Size Female to 15 mm; male to 10 mm.
Web None.
Habitat Under stones and logs; in and around buildings (in crevices).
Range Europe; introduced to Japan, N and S America, S Africa, Australia and New Zealand.
Season Adults all year.

SNEAK SPIDER *Harpactea hombergi*

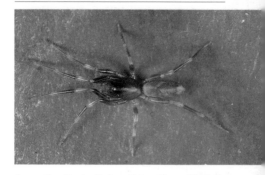

A small, slim-bodied spider with a blackish carapace and a grey-brown abdomen. The legs are banded black and brown. It lives in a silken cell and emerges to hunt small insects at night, advancing in a furtive way with its long first pair of legs held out in front. In this way, the spider measures the size of any insect encountered and withdraws in a flash if it turns out to be potentially dangerous.

Size Female to 7 mm; male to 6 mm.
Web None.
Habitat In woods: beneath loose bark of trees, under stones and among piles of dried vegetation.
Range Most of Europe.
Season Adults probably all year; mating during spring.

TUBE-WEB SPIDER *Segestria florentina*

An impressive spider seen at night or only briefly when it rushes to intercept an insect at the entrance to its web. The black, cigar-shaped body and iridescent green mouthparts are unmistakable. The web occupies a hole in a wall or tree trunk and is recognised by the neat trip-lines which radiate out and communicate vibrations back to the spider. At night, the spider waits with each of its first six legs resting on one of the lines.

Size Female to 22 mm; male to 15 mm.
Web A simple tubular kind with radiating trip-lines.
Habitat Old walls, rocks, under stones and tree bark.
Range Cosmopolitan, including Europe, Argentina and New Zealand.
Season In Europe, adults June–November.

SNAKE'S BACK SPIDER *Segestria senoculata*

A species recognised by a line of large black spots on a grey abdomen. The pattern is reminiscent of a snake's back, e.g. an adder or viper. The rather long carapace is dark glossy brown and the legs are pale brown. This spider lives in a tubular retreat in a crevice or under stones. It waits near the entrance and drags its insect prey back into the retreat. Sometimes it uses holes left by wood-boring insects.

Size	Female to 10 mm; male to 9 mm.
Web	Trip-lines radiate from the entrance to a silk-lined retreat.
Habitat	Old walls, rocks and the rugged bark of trees.
Range	Europe and much of Asia to Japan.
Season	Adults May–November.

TINY HOUSE SPIDER *Oonops domesticus*

A very small, orange-pink spider with six eyes in two groups. It rests during the day in a loose silk cell but at night may be seen walking stealthily on the walls of a house, with characteristic short rushes. This minute species attacks microscopic insects such as book lice, but if a potential victim turns out to be too large, the spider darts backwards. Batches of just two pink eggs are laid in summer in the mother's silk cell.

Size	Female to 2 mm; male to 1.5 mm.
Web	None, but sometimes found in the web of other spiders.
Habitat	Buildings, birds' nests, under stones and bark.
Range	Most of Europe.
Season	Adults probably in all seasons.

LACE-WEB WEAVERS

Lace-web spiders spin an ultra-fine, woolly silk. It is 'back-combed' by a rear leg from a field of fine openings (cribellum) in front of the spinnerets. Many lace-webs have a characteristic zigzag appearance and the silk may look bluish when fresh. The fuzzy texture of the silk usually lacks sticky globules but it is remarkably good at snagging the legs of insects.

Cribellate spiders form a group of more than a dozen families, including Dictynidae, Eresidae, Amaurobiidae, Deinopidae and Uloboridae. Their webs are mostly sheet-like but the uloborids spin orb-webs and the deinopids make expandable nets.

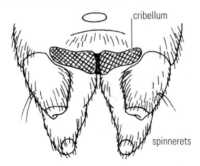

cribellum

spinnerets

LADYBIRD SPIDER *Eresus walckenaerius*

With four white-edged, black spots on a bright red abdomen, the male (left) resembles a ladybird. The front legs are black and white but the rear legs are orange. The carapace is velvety blue-black, as is the entire body and legs of the much larger female (right). She usually hides under stones but the male can be seen on sunny spring days running across open ground, in search of a mate. The diet is mostly beetles.

Size Female to 20 mm; male to 10 mm.
Web An irregular lace-like sheet, with a retreat.
Habitat Mediterranean vegetation and heather.
Range SE Europe and SW Asia.
Season Adult females probably all year; males active March–July.

VELVET SPIDER *Stegodyphus lineatus*

A thicket spider with a velvety appearance. The oval abdomen is striped grey and white and the legs are short and stout. This spider is difficult to see because it is reluctant to emerge from its impenetrable web built among spiny bushes. But its diet is easy to determine because numbers of dry, sucked insect bodies remain attached to the web for many weeks. They include beetles, dragonflies and earwigs.

Size	Female to 15 mm; male to 8 mm.
Web	A dense and woolly tube. It is closed when young are present and difficult to prize apart.
Habitat	Scrub and waysides; frequent on gorse bushes.
Range	S Europe and N Africa.
Season	Adult females all year; males April–October.

STAR-WEB SPIDER Uroctea durandi

This species has a black, heart-shaped abdomen with five yellow spots. The carapace has a 'snout' at the front and the eyes form a compact group. The abdomen overhangs the carapace, giving it a hunch-backed appearance. The legs are short. This spider is rarely seen in the open and usually remains under a stone, behind its characteristic star-shaped web. The old bodies of prey (ants, beetles and millipedes) adhere to the web.

Size Female to 12 mm; male to 8 mm.
Web A small, dense sheet with scalloped corners fastened to the underside of a stone.
Habitat Old walls and stony Mediterranean scrub.
Range S Europe and N Africa.
Season Adult females all year; males April–July.

NET-CASTING SPIDER *Deinopis longipes*

During the day, this weird spider resembles a twig. At night, it hangs upside down and holds a net, about the size of a small postage stamp, in its front legs. With amazing speed, the spider spreads the net to catch insects as they crawl or even fly past. Also called the Ogre-faced Spider, it has two huge front eyes that enable it to see in the darkness of the forest at night. Both male and female have long legs and a grey-brown body.

Size	Female to 15 mm; male to 10 mm.
Web	A small expandable net held by the front legs.
Habitat	Trees and rocks in tropical forest, in gardens and on walls.
Range	Central America from Mexico to Panama.
Season	Adults probably during warm, rainy seasons.

59

FEATHER-LEGGED WEAVER *Uloborus plumipes*

This spider has a short, humped abdomen and the first two legs are plumed and much longer and stronger than the others. It sits in perfect camouflage among a string of old insect bodies on a band of silk across the web's hub. This species, and others in the genus *Uloborus*, lacks venom glands and so prey is wrapped in silk and eaten alive.

Size Female to 6 mm; male to 4 mm.
Web An orb with a lace-like hub; often built in the fork of a dead branch.
Habitat Shrubs in shady places and gardens; also around rocks.
Range Europe, Africa and Asia; frequent on islands.
Season Adults probably all year.

TRIANGLE-WEAVER *Hyptiotes paradoxus*

Usually ginger-brown, the Triangle-weaver has a hunched appearance with short stout legs and eyes in a compact group. The male is smaller than the female but his palps are noticeably large. The web resembles a section of an orb-web but it operates differently. The spider's body forms a living link in the bridge thread; when an insect touches the web, the spider lets out more silk causing the web to collapse around it.

Size Female to 7 mm; male to 4 mm.
Web A triangle diverging from a bridge thread; usually built 1.5 m or more above ground.
Habitat Evergreen trees and shrubs in woodland.
Range Europe and W Asia.
Season Adults June–September.

HACKLED-WEB WEAVER *Dictyna arundinacea*

A small, furry, pale brown species with two white bands on the carapace. The abdomen has a dark brown central band broken towards the rear. The little web is positioned at the head of a grass stem or dried twig. It is criss-crossed with wavy and woolly silk produced through a special sieve-like plate just in front of the spider's spinnerets. The male's jaws are large. During summer the two sexes may be found together.

Size	Female to 3.5 mm; male to 2.5 mm.
Web	A lace-like web with a tubular retreat.
Habitat	Grassland, heather and gorse.
Range	Europe and much of Asia.
Season	Adults April–August.

Leaf Lace-weaver *Nigma puella*

Rarely seen unless the leaves on which it lives are carefully examined. The female of this furry little spider has a dark carapace with a central grey band and the abdomen is mostly pale green with a pattern of purple and green barring. Often a red dot or stripe appears on the abdomen. The male is reddish-brown overall, but the abdomen may be orange-pink with a darker central band.

Size Female to 3 mm; male to 2.5 mm.
Web A lace-like web built flat against a large, soft leaf.
Habitat Woodland and gardens, on trees and bushes.
Range Europe (especially SW) and N Africa.
Season Adults April–September.

WINDOW LACE-WEAVER *Amaurobius fenestralis*

A distinctive species with a glossy brown carapace and legs, and a velvety abdomen with a dark, wedge-shaped cardiac mark at the front surrounded by cream. The male is slimmer than the female. This species is quite familiar in Europe because it occurs around the windows of buildings and under old pots. The eggs are laid inside the web and the dead mother may be eaten by her spiderlings.

Size Female to 10 mm; male to 7 mm.
Web A lace-like web built around the entrance to a hole or crevice.
Habitat Woodland; on rocks, tree trunks, walls and around windows.
Range Europe and W Asia.
Season Adult females all year; males June–November.

BLACK LACE-WEAVER *Amaurobius ferox*

A sinister-looking species which appears to have a ghostly pattern on the abdomen. The carapace is dark, glossy brown and the abdomen and legs are blackish. The male is slimmer than the female but otherwise similar. This nocturnal spider spins its web using a hind leg to comb the silk out. Prey is also captured during the day. Vibrations from a tuning fork can bring a response from the spider.

Size Female to 16 mm; male to 12 mm.
Web An irregular, lace-like web around a funnel.
Habitat Woodland and gardens; under loose bark, stones and logs; in cellars and rubbish dumps.
Range Europe and N America; now in New Zealand.
Season Adult females all year; males in spring and autumn.

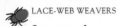

SOUTHERN LACE-WEAVER *Badumna longinqua*

A rather hairy, grey-brown spider. The abdomen has a central cardiac mark and a series of streaks on either side. The male is slimmer than the female but otherwise similar. When first spun, the web shows the zigzag construction so common in lace-web weavers but as the web is added to, it resembles a dusty sheet web. At night, the spider takes up position at the mouth of its retreat.

Size	Female to 12 mm; male to 10 mm.
Web	An irregular, lace-like web with a tubular retreat.
Habitat	Rock faces, walls and corners of houses, hedges and shrubs.
Range	New Zealand, Australia and USA.
Season	Adult females all year; males September–March.

Black Hole Spider *Kukulcania hibernalis*

An elegant, velvety, blue-black or brown species. The carapace is noticeably pointed and the eight eyes form a compact group on a small hump. The males have long palps and longer legs than the females. By day this spider hides in a tubular, silk-lined retreat in a hole. It is a long-lived species which survives for up to five years; young specimens are paler than older ones.

Size Female to 18 mm; male to 10 mm.
Web Many long strands of frilly silk radiate from the retreat's mouth.
Habitat Rocks, sand dunes, old walls and buildings.
Range Southern N America.
Season Adults probably all year.

KNOBBLE SPIDER *Zoropsis spinimana*

A handsome species, resembling a wolf spider (pp.158–166), with a rich brown carapace and a paler abdomen with a central wedge-shaped cardiac mark in the first half. The legs are dark towards the ends and pale towards the base. The eight eyes are similar in size. The male is slimmer than the female; the two are often found together under a stone or the peeling bark of a tree. During the winter this spider may seek refuge in a house.

Size Female to 21 mm; male to 14 mm.
Web A white, irregular lace-like sheet with a retreat.
Habitat Under bark, stones and in leaf litter.
Range SW Europe and N Africa.
Season Adult males most active in autumn; females with egg sacs occur in winter and early spring.

LAMPSHADE-WEAVER *Hypochilus gertschi*

This group of pale, long-legged spiders is intermediate in evolutionary terms between the 'tarantula' and 'true spider' divisions. The primitive features of *Hypochilus* include two pairs of book lungs (see p.20) but the fangs are not primitive as they close together. The spider hangs upside down in its strange, meshed web which is often built against an overhanging rock. Trapped insects are pulled through the web.

Size Female to 22 mm; male to 14 mm.
Web A 'lampshade' built of lace-like silk.
Habitat Rocks, cliff-faces and shallow caves in forest.
Range Eastern N America: Virginia and West Virginia.
Season Adult females probably all year; males
June–November.

JUNGLE LACE-WEAVER *Psechrus argentatus*

This spider's slim abdomen has a white line running along its underside. As it hangs upside down in its dome web, the white line may be seen from above but, at the slightest disturbance, the spider disappears into its retreat. The strongly-banded legs are long, particularly the two front pairs. The male and female are quite similar in appearance. The female carries the eggs in her jaws.

Size Female to 20 mm; male to 17 mm.
Web A large domed sheet of lace-like silk, with a funnel retreat.
Habitat Tropical forest; among branches or rocks and along tracks.
Range Malaysia, Indonesia and Queensland.
Season Adults probably all year.

Tangle- and Sheet-web Weavers

The tangle-web weavers belong to a single, large family (Theridiidae) also known as the comb-footed spiders. Small to medium-sized spiders, the females tend to have globular abdomens and are usually bigger than the males. They have eight small eyes. Many of the most venomous species belong to this family, e.g. Black Widow and Red Back spiders.

The sheet-web weavers are a group of about a dozen families. The family Linyphiidae contains the money or dwarf spiders. They spin small sheet webs in which the spider runs upside down on the underside. The Agelenidae contains larger species which mostly run on the top side of the sheet. Spiders in both families have eight eyes and males are not much smaller than females.

MOTHERCARE SPIDER *Theridion sisyphium*

This small spider has a rounded abdomen patterned brown, orange and white. The carapace is low and the eight eyes are arranged in two rows. On the final segment of the fourth pair of legs, a 'comb' of spines, characteristic of the family of tangle weavers, is used for flinging gummy silk over insect prey. This species is unusual in that the young are cared for and allowed to feed from the mother's mouth.

Size   Female to 4 mm; male to 3 mm.
Web   A tangle of threads around a conical retreat.
Habitat   Low plants in grassland, heathland and scrub.
Range   Europe and much of Asia.
Season   Adults May–August.

PALLID SPIDER *Paidiscura pallens*

The abdomen of this tiny spider is variable in colour and ranges from pale yellow to brown. The carapace is usually pale brown but has a dark central band. The male is darker than the female. These spiders construct their little webs on the underside of leaves and the mother spider suspends her huge, spiky egg sacs, which are much larger than she is, among the threads of the web.

Size	Female to 1.75 mm; male to 1.5 mm.
Web	A tangle of threads under a leaf, e.g. oak.
Habitat	Woodland and gardens; lower branches of trees and bushes.
Range	Europe and much of Asia.
Season	Adult males May–August; females probably all year.

73

GLASSHOUSE SPIDER *Achaearanea tepidariorum*

A domestic spider with a globular, grey-brown or blackish abdomen marked with pale chevrons. The carapace is yellowish and the legs are partly orange. It hangs upside down in its web; the outer threads are taut and beaded with glue, and if an insect gets stuck, it is jerked off the ground. The pear-shaped egg sacs are suspended in the web.

Size Female to 10 mm; male to 5 mm.
Web A tangle of threads without a purpose-built retreat.
Habitat In cold climates in buildings and glasshouses; in warm climates on trees, shrubs, bridges and fences.
Range Cosmopolitan; probably native to S America.
Season Adults and eggs all year.

DEW-DROP SPIDER *Argyrodes elevatus*

A small, silvery-brown spider with a high, domed abdomen. It usually lives in the webs of other, larger spiders ('hosts') and steals their food. Such spiders are called kleptoparasites. They feed on small insects caught in the web or join the host in eating a large insect. Large numbers of them in a web can seriously reduce the host's food. Sometimes the host tolerates them but at other times evicts them.

Size Female to 3 mm; male to 2 mm.
Web Uses the webs of other spiders such as dome-weavers (*Cyrtophora*) (pp.137–8) and golden orb-weavers (*Nephila*) (pp.103–8).
Habitat Forest, waysides and gardens.
Range Central and S America and southern USA.
Season Adults all year.

H-WEB SPIDER *Episinus algericus*

Recognised by its abdomen which is wider behind than in front. The legs are pale brown without any banding. The species is remarkable for its economical use of silk producing a web of minimal proportions. However, by virtue of placing the strands of the web in a strategic spot, such as at a plant's branching point, the spider is efficient at catching ants and other small insects.

Size Female to 5 mm; male to 4 mm.
Web A simple 'H'; the spider hangs upside down at the centre of four threads; the two held by the front legs (trap threads) have sticky globules.
Habitat Among bushes and climbing shrubs.
Range SW Europe and N Africa.
Season Adults March–July.

RABBIT HUTCH SPIDER *Steatoda bipunctata*

The female is rounded and glossy-brown with variable white bands across and around the abdomen. The male is darker and slimmer. Found in many kinds of buildings, this species shows a preference for rabbit hutches and chicken coops where there is plenty of insect prey. Here the spiders can become very numerous. Often they sit in crevices near their web.

Size	Female to 8 mm; male to 5 mm.
Web	A tangle-web, with taut threads below bearing sticky globules.
Habitat	Buildings, outbuildings and rubbish dumps.
Range	Europe and N America.
Season	Adult females all year; males in summer and autumn.

CELLAR SPIDER *Steatoda grossa*

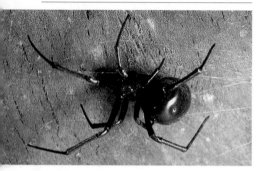

A black, or purplish-brown, rounded spider with a vague pattern of pale markings on the abdomen (a semicircle and three spots). The body never has any red markings. The male's abdomen has a series of white marks. Like some of the other larger tangle weavers, this species is mildly venomous. White egg sacs, like balls of cotton wool, are suspended among the web. After the spiderlings emerge, they share the mother's insect prey.

Size Female to 10 mm; male to 6 mm.
Web A tangle-web, with taut threads below bearing sticky globules.
Habitat Cellars, outbuildings, hollow trees and caves.
Range Cosmopolitan: Europe, Asia, N and S America.
Season Adult females all year; males in summer.

FALSE WIDOW SPIDER *Steatoda paykullianus*

This species resembles the notorious Black Widow Spider (p.80). The carapace, legs and abdomen are blackish. There is an orange, red or yellow band at the front of the abdomen and often also along the centre. The male is slimmer than the female. The web operates as a kind of 'spring-trap'. The bite of the adult female is mildly venomous.

Size	Female to 15 mm; male to 7 mm.
Web	A tangle-web with taut threads below bearing sticky globules.
Habitat	Under rocks and stones, in buildings and plantations.
Range	S Europe, N Africa and W Asia.
Season	Adult females probably all year; males in spring and autumn.

BLACK WIDOW SPIDER *Latrodectus mactans*

The highly venomous Black Widow Spider is unmistakable. About the size of a thumbnail, the female is satin-black and usually has a bright red 'hourglass' marking on the underside. The pale male is much smaller and does not bite. The female can overcome large creatures such as scorpions by throwing gummy silk at them as they struggle in the web. The round egg sac is brown and papery.

Size Female to 16 mm; male to 5 mm.
Web A tangle-web with taut threads below bearing sticky globules.
Habitat Buildings, plantations and stony places.
Range Southern USA and other warm regions of the world.
Season Depends on location.

RED-BACK SPIDER *Latrodectus hasselti*

The notorious Red-back of Australia, with its very painful bite, is the equivalent of the Black Widow in N America. It is satin-black or dark brown and is recognised by a broad, or slender, red stripe on the upper surface of the abdomen. The pale brown male is much smaller and does not bite. The white, spherical egg sacs, about the size of the female, are suspended in the web or placed in a tubular retreat.

Size Female to 14 mm; male to 4 mm.
Web A tangle-web with taut threads below bearing sticky globules.
Habitat Dry, stony regions and buildings.
Range Gulf Region and Australia; introduced to New Zealand and Japan.
Season Adults probably all year.

KATIPO *Latrodectus katipo*

The female Katipo is black with a red stripe across the abdomen. The much smaller male has a brown carapace with a central black band and a white abdomen with two irregular black bands enclosing a string of orange, diamond-shaped patches. The spider's web is built close to the ground and catches mostly beetles – many of them larger than the spider itself. Often the 'larder' contains a number of insects hauled above the ground.

Size	Female to 10 mm; male to 4 mm.
Web	A tangle-web with some taut threads bearing sticky globules.
Habitat	Coastal dunes, especially among marram grass.
Range	New Zealand (N Island and northern part of S Island).
Season	Adult females probably all year; males September–November.

MALMIGNATTE *Latrodectus tredecimguttatus*

An attractive species of the tangle-web group related to the Black Widow and Red-back spiders (pp.80 & 81). The fully-grown adult females have a round, black abdomen beautifully marked with thirteen red spots. The male is smaller and marked with white. A dark variety of this species, found widely in the Mediterranean, may have red bars on the underside but lacks the thirteen red spots.

Size Female to 15 mm; male to 7 mm.
Web A tangle-web with taut threads bearing sticky globules, built among stones and shrubs.
Habitat Stony areas with Mediterranean scrub.
Range S Europe (typical spotted form in Corsica).
Season Adult females May–November; males June–July.

BROWN WIDOW SPIDER *Latrodectus geometricus*

This tangle-web weaver is a house spider in many warm countries. The adult female is usually brown but varies from almost black, to cream with brown markings, and to bluish-grey. There is usually an orange 'hourglass' marking on the underside. The bite may be painful but is not highly poisonous. The male is small and lacks the hourglass marking. A web may contain a number of spiky egg sacs.

Size	Female to 12 mm; male to 5 mm.
Web	An untidy tangle-web with taut threads bearing sticky globules.
Habitat	Buildings: corners of rooms, under ledges; in gardens on opuntia and cactus.
Range	Cosmopolitan in warm countries.
Season	Adults all year.

RED AND WHITE SPIDER *Enoplognatha ovata*

A small, pretty spider often found in gardens. The carapace is glossy olive-brown and the legs are pale. The female has three different morphological varieties: the white or yellow abdomen has: (1) rows of spots; (2) a wide red mark; or (3) two red stripes. The male's jaws are huge. This spider lives in a curled-up leaf beside its web. The egg sac (shown here) is large, bluish and woolly, and is guarded under the cover of a leaf.

Size Female to 7 mm; male to 5 mm.
Web A small tangle-web constructed among leaves.
Habitat Gardens and rank grass with weeds and shrubs.
Range Europe; introduced to N America.
Season Adults June–August.

HAMMOCK-WEB SPIDER *Linyphia triangularis*

The sheet-webs of this species are a familiar sight on bushes in Europe. The spider's abdomen is longer than wide and appears shiny dark brown with white or yellow streaks. The legs are slender. This spider hangs upside down below its sheet and, in summer, both male and female can be found in the same web. If an insect gets entangled, it is grabbed and pulled through the sheet to be devoured below.

Size Female to 7 mm; male to 6 mm.
Web A slightly domed sheet with scaffolding threads above and below.
Habitat Shrubs in woodland and grassland.
Range Europe and much of Asia.
Season Adults June–October.

87

PLATFORM-WEB SPIDER *Neriene peltata*

This small, rather slender, brown and cream sheet-weaver is common along many bushy paths and waysides. The body of both the male and female is decorated by a dark brown indented central band, flanked on either side by a cream band. This spider hangs upside down on the underside of its sheet and does not build any retreat. On dewy mornings huge numbers of the webs can be seen.

Size	Female to 4 mm; male to 3 mm.
Web	A modest sheet with a superstructure of fine threads.
Habitat	Bushes, hedges and the lower branches of trees.
Range	Europe and much of Asia to Japan.
Season	Adults April–October.

88

MONEY SPIDER *Hypomma bituberculatum*

One of some 2000 tiny species (most about 2–3 mm) that are called 'money spiders' because they are supposed to bring luck. The family is especially common in temperate and cooler regions of the northern hemisphere. Most money spiders are 'aeronauts', i.e. they can travel through the air attached to lines of silk. Many species build small sheet-webs on the ground, in, for example, depressions made by animal hooves.

Size   Female to 3 mm; male to 2.5 mm.
Web   A small, rough sheet with scaffolding threads above and below.
Habitat   In wet meadows, beside ponds and streams.
Range   Europe and much of Asia to Japan.
Season   Adults April–October.

INVISIBLE SPIDER *Drapetisca socialis*

Another of the so-called money spiders. The carapace is olive-green and marked with dark striae. The abdomen is generally dark with a silvery area near the front. The legs are banded. This spider moves around on trees and leaves and also spins a web. On a tree trunk, it appears to sit with its legs outstretched but not touching the bark because the extremely fine web is usually visible only when the sun catches it at the right angle.

Size   Female to 4 mm; male to 3 mm.
Web   A small, fine sheet on a tree trunk.
Habitat   Woodland, especially beech, birch and conifers.
Range   Europe and much of Asia.
Season   Adults June–November.

GRASS FUNNEL-WEAVER *Agelena labyrinthica*

This spider has an olive-grey, chevron-patterned abdomen and a brown carapace with three pale bands. The end of the abdomen has two long, flexible spinnerets. Prey landing on the sheet-web brings the spider out of its retreat; after orientating itself towards the prey, the spider dashes out to capture it and drag it back. Though the web may be described as a funnel-web, this spider is unrelated to the Sydney Funnel-web Spider (p.26).

Size Female to 15 mm; male to 10 mm.
Web A large sheet with vertical threads and a funnel-like retreat.
Habitat In grass and on shrubs such as bramble.
Range Europe and much of Asia to Japan.
Season Adults June–August.

MOTHERPHAGE SPIDER *Coelotes terrestris*

Rarely seen because it usually lives under fallen logs and other such places. The carapace and legs are glossy dark brown and the abdomen is dark grey with a vague pattern of chevrons. The young spiders receive a great deal of maternal care until, in her second autumn, the mother dies and a process of self-digestion takes over. The spiderlings then feed on the corpse, thus recycling the nutrients.

Size Female to 15 mm; male to 12 mm.
Web An irregular sheet with a tube-like retreat into the ground.
Habitat Woodlands, often in mountainous regions.
Range Europe and W Asia.
Season Adult males June–November; females all year.

COMMON HOUSE SPIDER *Tegenaria domestica*

Generally unwelcome because of the dusty sheet-webs or 'cobwebs' which it leaves in the corners of rooms and against windows. It is banded grey-brown on the legs and carapace and has a series of chevrons on the abdomen. The spider emerges from its retreat to deal with insects that land on the web, running on the upper surface. The male (shown here) and female may live together during the breeding season.

Size	Female to 12 mm; male to 10 mm.
Web	An untidy sheet with a funnel-shaped retreat.
Habitat	Buildings, caves and hollow trees.
Range	Cosmopolitan.
Season	Adults probably all year.

CARDINAL SPIDER *Tegenaria parietina*

This long-legged species is one of the largest of the European house spiders. The adult male (shown here) has a leg span reaching 13 cm. The female has shorter legs but the body is larger. These spiders are generally pale in colour but the first pair of legs are characteristically dark brown on the first segment (especially the male's). Like other Tegenarias, the mother remains with the egg sac until the spiderlings emerge and disperse.

Size   Female to 20 mm; male to 15 mm.
Web   A large, untidy sheet or cobweb with a funnel retreat.
Habitat   Old buildings, caves and hollow trees.
Range   Europe, N Africa and W Asia.
Season   Adults June–November.

COBWEB SPIDER *Tegenaria gigantea*

A very common sheet-weaver which, perhaps more than any other species of spider, is responsible for arachnophobia. In the home, this species is familiar as the grey-brown, leggy spider which runs quickly and gets trapped in baths. Usually this is the male who abandons web-building to search for a mate. He often lives with the female for some weeks but then dies and she eats him.

Size Female to 16 mm; male to 14 mm.
Web An untidy sheet or cobweb with a funnel-shaped retreat.
Habitat Buildings, hollow trees, caves and under debris.
Range Europe and N America.
Season Adult females all year; males in summer and autumn.

YARD SPIDER *Tegenaria agrestis*

A mottled, grey-brown spider, greenish in certain light. It is a European species which has spread to the Pacific NW of the USA where it has become known for its aggressiveness; curiously it bites humans more frequently there than it does in Europe. In Europe it builds its sheet-web in wasteland whereas in N America it is found typically in backyards and buildings – perhaps places where it has more contact with humans.

Size   Female to 15 mm; male to 10 mm.
Web   A rough sheet with a funnel retreat, built among wood or other debris on the ground.
Habitat Gardens, yards, wasteland and open areas.
Range Europe and N America.
Season Adults June–November.

ORB-WEAVERS

Built by a large number of species, orb-webs are two-dimensional, vertical or horizontal structures; the largest, built by the golden orb-weavers, may be a metre wide and, with support threads, can span gaps from tree to tree. Fresh orb-webs are most efficient, so they are often rebuilt daily.

The main families of orb-weavers are the Araneidae, Tetragnathidae and Metidae. In most cases, the males are usually smaller than females; in some, males are far smaller.

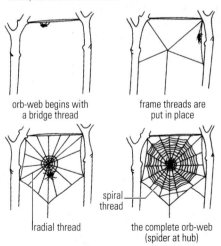

orb-web begins with a bridge thread

frame threads are put in place

radial thread

spiral thread

the complete orb-web (spider at hub)

Long-jawed Orb-weaver *Tetragnatha montana*

A slim-bodied, long-legged species with a brown carapace and striped abdomen, darker below than above. This spider is usually seen at the hub of its web in a long, thin, stretched-out posture. At other times, it rests with legs extended along a plant stem. Where the web is built near water, the diet is mostly aquatic insects. Both male and female have huge fangs with spurs to hold each other during mating; they are harmless to humans.

    Size Female to 12 mm; male to 9 mm.
    Web A lightly-built horizontal orb.
Habitat Streams, ponds, marshes, damp woods and
          shady roadside banks.
  Range Europe, N Africa, N America, Asia and Japan.
 Season Adults June–August.

COMMON ORB-WEAVER *Metellina segmentata*

One of the commonest spiders in Europe, appearing almost anywhere among vegetation. It is mostly pale brown and has a shield-like pattern on the abdomen. The legs are banded dark and pale and are relatively long in the smaller and slimmer, more orange-coloured male. During the mating season, the male may be seen waiting patiently in the upper part of the female's web.

Size Female to 8 mm; male to 6 mm.
Web A lightly-built vertical orb; the spider waits at the hub.
Habitat Woodland, heathland, gardens and scrub.
Range Europe, Asia and Canada.
Season Adults June–November.

ORCHARD ORB-WEAVER *Leucauge* sp.

A brightly-coloured tropical spider. The longish, silvery-white abdomen of the female has two slight humps at the front. It is striped yellow, green and black and is quite dark below. The legs are green but the carapace is brown. In the male, the legs are mostly brown and longer than those of the female; in both sexes the last two legs often have a fringe of curled hairs. The spider is usually seen hanging from the centre of its web.

Size	Female to 12 mm; male to 8 mm.
Web	An inclined orb with a network of threads beneath.
Habitat	Low vegetation in damp forests, neglected orchards and gardens; often near water.
Range	India and SE Asia to Queensland.
Season	Adults most frequent during rainy seasons.

CAVE ORB-WEAVER *Meta menardi*

This fine species almost always builds its web in very dark places. It has a rich, glossy brown carapace, spiny banded legs and a grey-brown, oval abdomen with a vague pattern of pale chevrons. The female constructs a large, white, globular egg sac which is pointed on top and suspended from the roof on a silk stalk. The male has longer legs and a slimmer abdomen.

Size Female to 16 mm; male to 12 mm.
Web A lightly-built vertical orb; often suspended from a roof.
Habitat Caves, mines, hollow trees, railway tunnels, drains, covered wells and corners of outbuildings.
Range Europe, Asia, Japan and N America.
Season Adults all year.

GIANT ORB-WEAVER *Nephila maculata*

With a leg span up to 15 cm, this is one of the largest orb-weavers in the world. The web, a metre wide and made of strong, golden silk, is built across the flight path of large insects. The female's dark, cigar-shaped abdomen may be spotted beneath and striped yellow above. The carapace is yellowish and the thin blackish legs and palps show some orange. The brown male is so small he can climb fearlessly over the female's body.

  Size Female to 45 mm; male to 8 mm.
  Web A huge vertical orb with a hub near the top.
 Habitat Tropical forests and gardens.
  Range India to S Japan and N Australia.
 Season Adult females all year; males during hot, humid seasons.

BATIK ORB-WEAVER *Nephila antipodiana*

This spider, one of the golden orb-weavers, has a strikingly-marked, yellow-spotted abdomen. The female's jaws are robust and the palps are black. She hangs head-down at the hub of her web, which is often built on telegraph wires, fully exposed to the sun, no matter how hot. The glossy brown male is much smaller than the female and during the mating season is often seen waiting in a corner of the web.

Size Female to 35 mm; male to 8 mm.
Web A large vertical orb, similar to that of the Giant Orb-weaver (p.103).
Habitat Gardens, roadsides and edges of mangrove swamps.
Range Malaysia, Thailand, Philippines and Indonesia.
Season Adult females all year; males during hot, humid seasons.

Golden Orb-weaver *Nephila clavipes*

A handsome species which builds a large web made with high-strength silk. The female sits at the web's hub and has conspicuous tufts of hair on the long legs (except the third pair). The carapace is grey or brown and the long abdomen is dark olive-brown with pairs of pale spots and often a pale border. The male is brown with darker legs. Like other species of the genus, it can repair damage to its web.

Size   Female to 35 mm; male to 10 mm.
Web   A large vertical orb, similar to that of the Giant Orb-weaver (p.103).
Habitat   Forests, swamps and shady gardens.
Range   SE USA, Caribbean, Central and S America.
Season   Adult females probably all year; males May–September.

AFRICAN GOLDEN ORB-WEAVER *Nephila senegalensis*

A large spider which hangs head-down in its web, often beside a line of old insect bodies. The female's dark, elongated abdomen is boldly marked with a white oblong ring enclosing white bars. The carapace is clothed with silvery hairs and the plumed legs are banded yellow and black. The male may be present in the female's web but can be mistaken for a kleptoparasitic spider (see p.75).

Size Female to 35 mm; male to 7 mm.
Web A large vertical orb, similar to that of the Giant Orb-weaver (p.103).
Habitat Edges of secondary forest and alongside tracks.
Range Sub-Saharan Africa, from Gambia to S Africa.
Season Adult females all year; males during hot, humid seasons.

MADAGASCAN ORB-WEAVER *Nephila inaurata*

Another large golden orb-weaving spider. The abdomen is long and somewhat conical in shape. The broad front of the abdomen is white and this gives way to a wedge-shaped marking of yellow and grey which continues to the end. The carapace and legs are black; the legs may have a tinge of red in the middle joints. The little brown male is inconspicuous.

Size Female to 35 mm; male to 5 mm.
Web A large vertical orb with a hub near the top.
Habitat Forest edges, along tracks and in gardens.
Range Central, E and S Africa; Madagascar and Seychelles.
Season Adult females probably all year; males during hot, humid seasons.

HERMIT ORB-WEAVER *Nephilengys cruentata*

A large, dark orb-weaver with a bright yellow or orange-red patch under the carapace. The legs are banded. This spider's silk is white and the webs are often found in groups. A tubular retreat is always built close to the web's hub and the spider emerges from the retreat to catch prey. The male is considerably smaller than the female.

Size Female to 25 mm; male to 5 mm.
Web An incomplete orb with a hub near the top joined to a retreat.
Habitat Edges of forest and mangroves; on tree trunks, rocks and buildings.
Range Sub-Saharan Africa and tropical S America.
Season Adult females all year; males during hot, humid seasons.

MALABAR ORB-WEAVER *Nephilengys malabarensis*

A bulky orb-weaver with a bright yellow or orange patch under the carapace and a further four similarly-coloured patches under the abdomen. The carapace is reddish-brown and the strong brown legs are rather short. The webs are often found in groups around buildings. If disturbed, these nocturnal spiders escape into their retreat, which is always close to the web's hub. The male is considerably smaller than the female.

Size Female to 20 mm; male to 5 mm.
Web A vertical orb with a hub near the top joined to a tubular retreat.
Habitat On trees, at the angles of branches and on buildings, especially under roof overhangs.
Range India and SE Asia to Australia and New Caledonia.
Season Adult females probably all year.

CROSS OR GARDEN SPIDER *Araneus diadematus*

One of the commonest spiders in the northern hemisphere. The female is recognised by the pale cross of white or yellow spots on the abdomen. The abdomen itself may be brown, red, black or beige. The carapace is brown with a dark central band. The eyes are in two rows and the spiny legs are banded light and dark. The smaller male is brown and has a white pattern on the abdomen.

Size   Female to 18 mm; male to 9 mm.
Web   A vertical orb; the spider sits at the hub or at the end of a signal thread.
Habitat   Woodland, scrub, roadsides and gardens.
Range   Europe and much of Asia to Japan; also parts of N America.
Season   Adults June–November.

ANGULAR ORB-WEAVER *Araneus angulatus*

A shapely species which exhibits a pair of humped or angular shoulder-like tubercles on the abdomen. The grey or buff abdomen overhangs the grey carapace and usually has a well-defined, leaf-like pattern on the back and a triangular mark between the tubercles. The spiny legs are grey with black bands. In the male, the angular corners of the abdomen are reduced.

Size Female to 20 mm; male to 10 mm.
Web A vertical orb, often sited across insect flight paths.
Habitat Woodland and heathland.
Range Europe and much of Asia.
Season Adults June–November.

FOUR-SPOT ORB-WEAVER *Araneus quadratus*

An attractive species usually found hiding in a silk retreat beside an orb-web in low vegetation. The female has a large, round abdomen coloured either yellow, green, red or brown and marked with four large, and other smaller, white spots. The male is banded on the body and legs and the abdomen is a rich brown with white markings. This spider feeds mostly on jumping insects such as grasshoppers.

Size Female to 20 mm; male to 9 mm.
Web A vertical orb, built low down among ground vegetation.
Habitat Grassland, heathland and scrub.
Range Europe and much of Asia.
Season Adults June–November.

STRAWBERRY SPIDER *Araneus alsine*

A beautiful species in which the female's abdomen resembles a strawberry. The colour varies from pale orange to purplish-red and is marked by many small yellow spots. The legs and carapace are orange-brown. The smaller male resembles the female but is darker and slimmer. This spider lives near the web in a retreat which is usually made from one or two dried leaves forming an upside-down cone.

   Size Female to 12 mm; male to 7 mm.
   Web A vertical orb, built low down among grass.
Habitat Grassland, woodland clearings.
   Range Europe and much of Asia.
 Season Adults June–November.

PYRAMID ORB-WEAVER *Araneus marmoreus var. pyramidatus*

A distinctive orb-weaving spider recognised by a dark, pyramid-shaped marking at the back of the female's cream or orange abdomen. The abdomen overhangs the carapace which is grey-brown. The legs are pale yellow-white with dark bands. The smaller, darker male lacks the pyramid marking but has a pale, indented central band in the first half of the abdomen.

Size	Female to 16 mm; male to 8 mm.
Web	A vertical orb with a signal line from the hub to a retreat of several leaves fastened together.
Habitat	Tall meadows and waterside vegetation; often on trees.
Range	Europe, much of Asia and N America.
Season	Adults June–November.

GREAT GARDEN SPIDER *Eriophora transmarina*

A fine Australian species which spins a large, immaculate orb-web. The female is heavily built and furry; the male is also large. The colour is usually cream or beige but the abdomen may have a darker leaf pattern or a pair of white spots or a white 'arrowhead' design. The legs can be partly rusty-red. This nocturnal spider feeds mostly on moths; it removes the web at dawn and passes the day among leaves with legs held tight.

Size Female to 28 mm; male to 20 mm.
Web A large vertical orb often built well above ground and across trails or streams.
Habitat Suburban gardens, woodland and bushland.
Range Australia, New Guinea and New Zealand.
Season Adults October–May.

117

KIWI GARDEN SPIDER *Eriophora pustulosa*

An orb-weaver with a wide variety of colour patterns. These range from a white 'leaf' design on top of a brown abdomen (female) to mixtures of grey, black, yellow or brown. Fortunately, the spider can always be recognised by the angular 'shoulders' and five tubercles at the end of the abdomen. In all colour patterns, the legs are banded dark and pale. The male is usually grey. The green egg sac is attached to a twig near the web.

Size Female to 12 mm; male to 10 mm.
Web A vertical orb built among shrubs.
Habitat Suburban gardens, woodland and bushland.
Range Southern Australia, New Zealand and Pacific Islands.
Season Adults November–May.

CANOPY ORB-WEAVER *Parawixia hypocrita*

This nocturnal spider has a triangular abdomen with tubercles at the front and end. A triangular, dark brown band with indented sides occupies the upper surface of the abdomen. The carapace and legs are reddish-brown. Apart from size, the male and female are alike. This spider sits at the centre of its web, hides in a rolled-leaf retreat or sits in the open, resembling a dead leaf.

Size Female to 15 mm; male to 7 mm.
Web A vertical orb built high off the ground, often in the forest canopy.
Habitat Tropical rainforest.
Range S and Central America, including Peru, Brazil, Panama and Costa Rica.
Season Adults probably most of the year.

119

ORIENTAL GARDEN SPIDER *Parawixia dehaani*

This nocturnal orb-weaver has acute shoulder-like tubercles on the abdomen but its coloration is variable. In its most elegant form, a sharp line between the tubercles divides the front part of the abdomen, which is rich brown, from the remainder of the abdomen which is silvery-white. The male is grey-brown. During the day, the spider hides in a leaf near the web. When disturbed, it drops to the ground and 'plays dead'.

Size Female to 20 mm; male to 10 mm.
Web A vertical, lightly-built orb.
Habitat Gardens and clearings.
Range SE Asia: India to New Guinea and Pacific Islands.
Season Adults probably most of the year.

BLACK AND YELLOW ARGIOPE *Argiope aurantia*

The female has a black abdomen boldly decorated with silvery-yellow or gold; the carapace is silvery. The long legs are black or banded dark brown and orange. During even the hottest days, the spider hangs head-down at the hub of the web built among low vegetation to catch insects such as crickets. The dark male has two pale bands on the abdomen. The brown egg sacs are pear-shaped.

Size	Female to 25 mm; male to 8 mm.
Web	A vertical orb; decorated above and below the centre with a single zigzag band of white silk.
Habitat	Damp grassland, roadsides and gardens.
Range	N and Central America.
Season	Adult males June–August; females until November.

SILVER ARGIOPE *Argiope argentata*

A pretty species with a neat web. The female is silvery on the carapace and front part of the abdomen, while the back of the abdomen has five prominent lobes and is decorated with silver and orange or yellow. This spider builds an orb-web near the ground where it catches mostly jumping insects. The small male is pale brown and has two dark bands along the abdomen. The flattened egg sac is somewhat star-shaped.

Size Female to 18 mm; male to 5 mm.
Web A vertical orb, usually decorated with four zigzag bands of white silk forming a cross.
Habitat Woods, gardens and scrubland.
Range Southern USA to Argentina.
Season Adult females all year; males in warm seasons.

BRUENNICHI'S ARGIOPE *Argiope bruennichi*

Sometimes called the Wasp Spider because of the black and yellow (and white) banding on the female's abdomen. The carapace is silvery and the legs are banded dark and pale. The low-built web traps jumping insects such as grasshoppers. The small pale brown male waits in the female's web and tries to mate as soon as her old skin is shed on the final moult. Sometimes the female kills him. The egg sac is large and fluffy.

Size	Female to 25 mm; male to 7 mm.
Web	A vertical orb; usually with a zigzag band.
Habitat	Grassy places, roadsides and woodland edges.
Range	Europe (as far N as S England), S Asia, China and Japan.
Season	Adults June–September.

BANDED ARGIOPE *Argiope trifasciata*

The female spider has a pearly and gold abdomen, pointed to the rear and crossed by ten to twelve dark lines. Underneath, the abdomen has a pair of yellow marks. The carapace is silvery and the legs are banded pale and dark. The male has a white abdomen and a yellowish-brown carapace and legs. The web is built near the ground and catches flying and jumping insects. The brown egg sac is flat above and rounded below.

Size	Female to 25 mm; male to 8 mm.
Web	A vertical orb, often with a zigzag band.
Habitat	Grassland, scrub and roadsides.
Range	Warm regions worldwide; rare in S Europe.
Season	Adult males in summer; females also through autumn.

GRAND ARGIOPE *Argiope aemula*

One of the largest of the orb-weaving Argiopes. The oval abdomen of the female, which has angular corners at the front, is yellowish-white and marked with many transverse lines, becoming darker towards the rear. The dark legs are vaguely banded. The small male is dark brown. The bodies of insects swathed in silk are often seen in the web.

Size Female to 28 mm; male to 6 mm.
Web A vertical orb; the zigzag bands may number from none to four.
Habitat Forest clearings, open grassy areas and roadsides.
Range India and SE Asia to Queensland and S Japan.
Season Adult females probably all year; males in warm, humid seasons.

LOBED ARGIOPE *Argiope lobata*

An impressive orb-weaver common in the Mediterranean. The female's beige or silvery abdomen has from six to nine lobes (the last may be long). The orb-webs of the females are built in summer and catch large flying insects. Later in the summer, the small, slim-bodied males appear in the female's web. The egg sac is large and pear-shaped.

Size Female to 25 mm; male to 8 mm.
Web A vertical orb (up to two metres above ground) often decorated with a zigzag band of silk.
Habitat Hot, dry scrub, roadsides and edges of woods.
Range S Europe, Africa, Middle East, S and SE Asia.
Season Adults April–November (northern hemisphere).

MULTI-COLOURED ARGIOPE *Argiope versicolor*

This colourful species has a yellow-, brown- and white-banded, pentagonal abdomen and a silvery carapace. Like some other Argiopes, the female appears to have just four legs as she sits at the hub of the web with two legs together extending along each of the arms of the stabilimentum (see below). The flat, oval, whitish egg sac has a papery texture and is usually suspended beside the web.

Size Female to 12 mm; male to 5 mm.
Web A vertical orb, with four zigzag bands forming a cross (the stabilimentum) around the centre.
Habitat Tropical forest edges and clearings.
Range SE Asia, including Malaysia, Indonesia and Vietnam.
Season Adults through most of the year.

St. Andrews Cross Spider *Argiope picta*

The female (seen below) has a shield-shaped, bright yellow abdomen with semicircular bands of pearly-white and black towards the rear. The small male (seen above) is brown. When courting the male sits on the opposite side of the web and lures the female onto a thread towards him. The greenish egg sacs are pear-shaped and are usually suspended in shrubbery near the web. Food is mostly flying insects.

Size	Female to 15 mm; male to 5 mm.
Web	A vertical orb; the zigzag bands around the hub are often incomplete.
Habitat	Forest edges, grassy areas and gardens.
Range	N Australia and Indonesia.
Season	Adult females probably all year; males in summer (Australia).

GREEN ORB-WEAVER *Araniella cucurbitina*

A small, green spider, common in many places but not often seen because it lives among leaves. In both sexes, the carapace and legs are glossy brown while the abdomen is bright green with some yellow and red markings underneath. Their legs are vaguely banded. The egg sac has a woolly appearance; it is guarded by the female until she dies but later drops to the ground together with the leaves in autumn.

Size	Female to 7 mm; male to 5 mm.
Web	A small, often distorted, orb, usually hidden among leaves.
Habitat	Woodland and gardens.
Range	Europe, N Africa and much of Asia to Japan.
Season	Adults June–November.

NEAT ORB-WEAVER *Mangora acalypha*

A small, neatly-marked spider which builds a finely-meshed web. The abdomen is white at the front and yellow at the back, with a bold pattern of black markings. The yellowish carapace, with a thin black line in the middle, is pear-shaped and high at the back. This spider has no retreat and sits at the web's hub waiting for prey. If disturbed it runs up a blade of grass or drops down on a thread.

Size Female to 6 mm; male to 4 mm.

Web A densely-woven orb (about 60 radial threads), rebuilt each morning.

Habitat Woodland edges and gardens; among shrubs and rank weeds.

Range Europe, N Africa and much of Asia.

Season Adults June–September.

131

GORSE ORB-WEAVER *Agalenatea redii*

A small, squat spider often found among thorny bushes. The rather furry, grey-brown female has a number of different morphological varieties: one has cream spots on the abdomen and another has a dark, wedge-shaped marking on the second half of the abdomen together with a series of chevrons. The male has a more triangular abdomen with a dark cardiac mark outlined in white.

Size Female to 9 mm; male to 6 mm.
Web A vertical orb with a small platform nearby, on which the spider waits.
Habitat Gorse, heather and scrub.
Range Europe, N Africa and much of Asia.
Season Adult females April–October; males until June.

Mountain Orb-weaver *Aculepeira ceropegia*

A fine species with a striking, cream-coloured, lobed pattern on the abdomen which is pointed at both ends. The spinnerets lie below the abdomen and are not at the rear. The carapace is brown and the legs are banded. The male is much darker: brown-black with some cream markings. The web is built near the ground and the sight of the spider sitting on its silk platform is quite remarkable.

Size Female to 16 mm; male to 9 mm.
Web An inclined orb with a small platform, on which the spider sits.
Habitat Meadows and stony mountainsides.
Range Europe, N Africa and much of Asia.
Season Adults May–August.

LABYRINTH ORB-WEAVER *Metepeira labyrinthea*

This spider's wide, brown abdomen is decorated with a bold, lobed leaf-like pattern of black and white markings tapering towards the rear. The carapace is brown and noticeably pale in the eye region. The spider's complicated web is often built among dead branches. The female spins a labyrinth of threads with a retreat behind the web, and stays in this most of the time.

Size	Female to 8 mm; male to 5 mm.
Web	A vertical orb plus a tangle web and a woven retreat.
Habitat	On shrubs, in grassland and edges of woodland.
Range	N, Central and S America.
Season	Adult females all year in Florida; males June–September.

BORDERED ORB-WEAVER *Neoscona adianta*

A small, pretty species which looks like a smaller version of the Mountain Orb-weaver (p.133). In both sexes the abdomen is grey or reddish-brown with a bold series of white or yellow triangles, edged in black, along the abdomen. Males are similar to females but have a slimmer abdomen. The web is spun on low vegetation; it usually has a damaged appearance.

Size Female to 9 mm; male to 6 mm.
Web A vertical orb with a small platform nearby, on which the spider waits.
Habitat Open woods, gorse, heather, scrub and around fences.
Range Europe, N Africa and much of Asia to Japan.
Season Adults June–September.

ORIENTAL DOME-WEAVER *Cyrtophora moluccensis*

This species builds a complicated web which can grow to impressive heights and often neighbouring webs are joined together. The spider hangs upside down below a central dome. The carapace of the female is pale grey and the legs are pale brown with some red or brown bands. The white and yellow abdomen has a pattern of black markings, including two dark-tipped humps near the front. The small male has a pale brown abdomen.

Size Female to 18 mm; male to 5 mm.
Web A finely-woven, dome-shaped platform with masses of support threads.
Habitat Forest edges and against fences and pylons.
Range India and SE Asia, including islands.
Season Adults most frequent during rainy seasons.

Six-humped Dome-weaver *Cyrtophora citricola*

This spider lives within the safety of a large, complex web built among bushes. The oblong, white and black or brown abdomen of the female has six prominent tubercles. Strings of egg sacs looking like debris are suspended vertically in the web; the spider often sits under the last cocoon, at the top of the dome. Large colonies of spiders may build their webs together, sharing support lines.

Size Female to 15 mm; male to 4 mm.
Web A finely-woven, dome-shaped platform with masses of support lines.
Habitat Gardens, waysides and scrub; often within tough, thorny plants such as cacti and aloes.
Range S Europe, Africa and S Asia.
Season Adult females all year; males in warm seasons.

BARK SPIDER *Caerostris sexcuspidata*

This strange spider has a pair of leathery protuberances on the abdomen, camouflaging it against tree bark. The eyes are on a bump at the front of the carapace which is overhung by the abdomen. A nocturnal species, it constructs its orb-web at night and dismantles it at dawn. During the day it rests immobile on a branch. It is not known whether the small adult male spins an orb-web.

Size	Female to 16 mm; male to 5 mm.
Web	A large orb with a long bridge line to spider's resting place.
Habitat	Thorn trees.
Range	S, central and E Africa; also Madagascar.
Season	Adult females probably all year; males probably in summer (S Africa).

SCORPION ORB-WEAVER *Arachnura scorpionioides*

The strange, elongate abdomen of this species has two horns at the front and a peculiar star-shaped tip at the end. When the spider closes its legs, in a hunched position, the effect is to imitate a dry twig. When alarmed, the end of the abdomen curls upwards like a scorpion's tail. Normally, the spider hangs upside down and looks just like a rolled leaf below a string of debris and camouflaged egg cocoons from the hub to the top of the web.

Size	Female to 15 mm; male to 3 mm (lacks tail).
Web	An inclined, lightly-built orb with a missing V-shaped sector.
Habitat	Forest, gardens, shrubbery, reeds and swamps.
Range	Sub-Saharan Africa and Madagascar.
Season	Adults may occur through most of the year.

TREE-STUMP ORB-WEAVER *Poltys illepidus*

A strictly nocturnal species. The female has a wide, dark brown abdomen covered with many weirdly-shaped protuberances which contribute to its camouflage. The carapace narrows in front and the legs are vaguely banded. The male is very dark and has a hunched appearance. During the day, after dismantling the web, the female sits tight with legs in, resembling part of a knobbly tree branch. The web is rebuilt each evening.

Size	Female to 12 mm; male to 6 mm.
Web	A densely-woven orb with many radial and spiral threads.
Habitat	Forest edges, tracks and gardens.
Range	SE Asia: India to Japan and NE Australia.
Season	Adults November–May (Australia).

ORNATE ORB-WEAVER *Herennia ornatissima*

An attractive species with a pearly, spotted abdomen which is flat and lobed in outline. The carapace is grey and orange. This spider's web is difficult to see because it lies parallel to the bark of a tree. Insects such as dragonflies do not see the web until too late when attempting to land. The female sits on a lace-like area near the hub of the web. The small male lacks the wide, ornate abdomen of the female.

Size Female to 15 mm; male to 6 mm.
Web A vertical orb lying a few millimetres over the surface of a tree or rock.
Habitat Tree trunks and rock faces in forested areas.
Range SE Asia; from India to New Guinea.
Season Adults usually occur during hot, humid seasons.

143

BANKSIDE ORB-WEAVER *Larinioides cornutus*

This species, usually found near water, has a pale abdomen decorated with a wide, dark grey, leaf-like pattern. The carapace is dark brown and banded along its length. The smaller male also has a well-defined pattern. The web catches mostly aquatic insects; building usually takes place in the evening and this is one of the few species that builds orb-webs throughout a cold winter.

Size	Female to 10 mm; male to 7 mm.
Web	A vertical orb; the spider waits in a connected retreat.
Habitat	Usually near water, on grasses and reeds.
Range	Europe, N America and much of Asia.
Season	Adult females probably all year; males April–September.

WALNUT ORB-WEAVER *Nuctenea umbratica*

A rich brown and rather flat-bodied species that hides during the day behind peeling bark or in cracks in woodwork. It emerges in the evening to sit at the hub of the web. The female has a wide, heart-shaped abdomen with a dark, leaf-like pattern. The slimmer-bodied male has a reputation for biting. The eggs are laid in a flattened ball surrounded by loose, woolly silk.

Size Female to 15 mm; male to 10 mm.
Web A vertical orb with a signal line connected to a retreat.
Habitat Woods and gardens; old trees and buildings.
Range Europe, N Africa and S Asia.
Season Adult males June–October; females probably all year.

145

MISSING SECTOR ORB-WEAVER *Zygiella x-notata*

A common species often found in a retreat in a window corner. It sits in touch with a line (the signal thread) which transmits vibrations from the web. During the mating season, the male tweaks the female's signal line to announce his arrival. The abdomen is silvery and the carapace and legs are banded. In cold climates, this is one of the few species that spins its webs through the winter.

Size Female to 9 mm; male to 6 mm.
Web A vertical orb with a signal line passing through a V-shaped missing sector.
Habitat Trees, rocks, walls and buildings.
Range N America, Europe and much of Asia; introduced to Argentina and Chile.
Season Adult females all year; males during summer.

DECOY ORB-WEAVER *Cyclosa insulana*

A master of subterfuge, this spider sits among a mass of dead insects and cast skins which are intended to confuse predators. The female's abdomen has a brown pattern and projects to the front and rear. The carapace is narrow at the front. When at rest, this spider sits with hunched legs surrounding the carapace. The small, dark male has a more spherical abdomen. The egg sacs are attached to leaves.

Size	Female to 10 mm; male to 5 mm.
Web	A vertical orb with a mass of frilly silk around the hub.
Habitat	Forest, gardens, wasteland and coastal areas.
Range	S Europe, Africa, Asia and Australia.
Season	Adults during early summer.

SPINY-BACKED ORB-WEAVER *Gasteracantha fornicata*

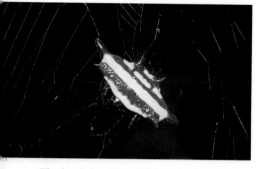

The female has a broad, flat, rectangular abdomen with six spines, two of them very prominent. The spines are probably for defence although the small male is not noticeably spiny. Several bright yellow or red bands cross the female's abdomen from side to side. The spinnerets are raised. The oval egg sac is covered with green fluffy silk and hidden beneath a leaf, close to the web.

Size Female to 10 mm (20 mm wide); male to 4 mm.
Web A lightly-built orb with long support lines.
Habitat Forest edges and gardens.
Range India and SE Asia to N Australia.
Season Adult females probably all year; males in hot, humid seasons.

HORNED ORB-WEAVER *Gasteracantha falcicornis*

Another of the spiny-backed spiders, the female has a hard, wide abdomen with stout, curved spines, sharp to the touch. The web is often built in spaces among trees, in full sunlight or in deep shade. It is usually spun at dawn and removed at dusk, the spider resting during the night on a few threads. In common with other spiny-backed spiders, small flecks of fluffy silk in the web probably help to attract flying insects.

Size	Female to 8 mm (wider than long); male to 3 mm.
Web	A lightly-built orb with long support lines.
Habitat	Tropical forest and gardens.
Range	E and S Africa.
Season	Adult females probably all year; males in hot, humid seasons.

KITE SPIDER *Gasteracantha versicolor*

Another spiny-backed orb-weaver. The female's orange and white abdomen is much wider than long and has six sharp spines, two of them very prominent. The carapace is short and so are the legs. In exposed positions, buffeted by winds, the spider sits at the web's hub with its black under-surface facing up and its bright upper-surface facing down. The dark male is minute and has only short spines.

Size Female to 12 mm; male to 4 mm.
Web A lightly-built orb across wide spaces.
Habitat Woodland and savannah; for example among Acacia trees.
Range Sub-Saharan Africa and Indian Ocean territories.
Season Adults November–March (S Africa).

LONG-HORNED ORB-WEAVER *Gasteracantha arcuata*

A spider with a distinctly odd appearance. The female sits in the middle of its web with two remarkably long, curved 'horns' on its abdomen facing out. No other spider has such long spines or horns. Their purpose remains a mystery. The abdomen is bright yellow with black spots; the horns and legs are black, and the carapace is dark brown. The male is smaller and lacks the long horns.

Size Female to 10 mm (25 mm across horns); male to 5 mm.
Web A lightly-built orb with a hole at the hub.
Habitat Tropical forest, beneath the branches of trees.
Range SE Asia from India to Indonesia.
Season Adult females probably all year; males during hot, humid seasons.

THORN SPIDER *Micrathena schreibersi*

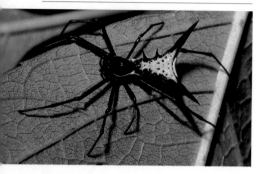

A shiny black species with a bright yellow abdomen sporting a pair of large spines. During the day, the spider hangs upside down from the hub of its web, looking like a spiny seed pod with warning coloration. Thorn spiders make unpleasant eating for birds but solitary wasps are serious enemies. The small male looks like an ant.

Size	Female to 12 mm; male to 4 mm.
Web	An inclined orb suspended above ground and more densely built than that of *Gasteracantha* (pp. 148-151).
Habitat	Forest and shady gardens.
Range	Central America (Nicaragua) to Brazil.
Season	Adult females probably all year; males in hot, humid seasons.

TRIANGULAR SPIDER *Arcys lancearius*

An unusual orb-weaver which has evolved in the direction of the crab spiders. It has abandoned web-building and ambushes its prey instead. Both male and female have a brightly-coloured, triangular-shaped abdomen, with two orange spots, and strong, spiky front legs which are held out to grasp passing insects such as ants. Day and night the spider lies in wait on leaves and flowers. The spherical egg sacs are orange-pink.

Size   Female to 9 mm; male to 5 mm.
Web   None.
Habitat   Among shrubs and trees in forests and gardens.
Range   E Australia, including Tasmania; also New Guinea.
Season   Adults November–March (Australia).

153

BOLAS SPIDER *Cladomelea longipes*

A renegade orb-weaver which has abandoned web-building and has taken to swinging a 'fishing line' with a sticky globule at the end. It does this at night from the outer branch of a shrub or tree. The spider catches flying male moths of a certain kind after luring them with its imitation of the female moth's pheromone (chemical attractant). The fat, orange body of the female spider is weirdly ornamented. The little males are rarely seen.

Size Female to 18 mm; male to 5 mm.
Web A single strand with one (or more) sticky globules at the end.
Habitat Forest and gardens.
Range W and E Africa.
Season Usually active during rainy seasons.

TWO-SPINED SPIDER *Poecilopachys australasia*

This gaudy spider is yellow and white with red and black and can darken or brighten its colours. However, it is rarely seen because it is nocturnal and sits under a leaf, with legs folded, during the day. The female builds an orb-web at dusk and dismantles it at dawn. The small adult male builds no web but conserves energy while waiting to mate with the female. The egg sac is spindle-shaped and protected by silk threads.

Size Female to 7 mm; male to 3 mm.
Web A vertical orb, up to two metres above ground.
Habitat Among shrubs, bushes and trees.
Range E Australia, New Guinea and Pacific islands.
Season Adult females probably all year; males reach maturity in early summer.

Costa Rican Orb-weaver *Verrucosa* sp.

A beautifully-marked spider with a glossy, triangular-shaped abdomen. Bright yellow shoulders enclose a deep red pattern which branches towards two of the black-tipped tubercles at the front of the abdomen. The rich brown carapace has a raised head region; the legs are black. The female spider is shown here together with its yellow, woolly egg cocoon which is attached to the underside of a large leaf. The male is unknown.

Size Female to 10 mm; male unknown.
Web A vertical orb.
Habitat Tropical rainforest; on large-leaved shrubs.
Range Costa Rica.
Season Adults probably during warm, humid seasons.

HUNTING SPIDERS

There are many hunting spiders belonging to a large number of families. Hunting spiders usually do not build webs but employ various tactics to catch their prey. Many rely on camouflage and surprise, others use speed and strength to overcome their victims. Often the females carry their egg cocoon with them and some also carry the babies after they hatch.

Typical families of hunting spiders include the wolf spiders (Lycosidae), wandering spiders (Ctenidae), nursery-web spiders (Pisauridae), huntsman spiders (Heteropodidae) and lynx spiders (Oxyopidae). Most have eight eyes; the wolf spiders in particular have a pair of large eyes facing forward.

EUROPEAN WOLF SPIDER *Lycosa narbonensis*

Like other wolf spiders, this large species is a ground hunter. The body and legs are grey, with dark chevrons on the abdomen. The mouthparts, and the area beneath the front legs, show a yellow or orange colour. The two large front eyes give good vision. Courtship involves waving and drumming the palps and legs. The mother carries her egg sac and, after hatching, the young ride on her back.

Size   Female to 28 mm; male to 20 mm.
Web   None.
Habitat   Grassland and open areas; the spider lives in a shallow burrow with a woven 'turret' around the entrance.
Range   S Europe.
Season   Adult females all year; males April–June.

RUSTIC WOLF SPIDER *Trochosa ruricola*

A medium-sized species which, like other wolf
spiders, has a long carapace and eyes in three rows
with two large eyes at the front. Both sexes are dark
brown and have a pale band that runs the length of
the carapace continuing to the first half of the
abdomen. The spider lives in a small burrow and
emerges to hunt at times during the day and night.
Courtship involves signalling with palps and legs.

Size	Female to 15 mm; male to 10 mm.
Web	None.
Habitat	Grassland, woodland, scrub and lawns.
Range	Europe and much of Asia to Japan.
Season	Adults April–June.

159

Fox Spider *Alopecosa cuneata*

This species has a broad, pale band along the carapace and abdomen. The band is more contrasting in the dark male (shown here) than in the brown female. Over the first half of the abdomen, in both sexes, the band widens to enclose a dark wedge-shaped cardiac mark. This spider hunts day or night and rests in a burrow. For a time after hatching, the mother carries 100 or so spiderlings on her back.

Size Female to 12 mm; male to 9 mm.
Web None.
Habitat Grassland and open places, especially on sandy and chalky soil.
Range Europe and much of Asia.
Season Adult females all year; males April–July.

GREY WOLF SPIDER *Alopecosa kochi*

One of the palest wolf spiders. The carapace is pale grey with contrasting dark grey sides. The legs and abdomen are a uniform pale grey though the abdomen has an indistinct outline in the middle towards the front. The eyes are quite large and occupy the front of the carapace. Like other wolf spiders, the mating ritual involves visual signals and touching with vibrating legs and palps.

Size	Female to 15 mm; male to 10 mm.
Web	None.
Habitat	Many types of wooded and open country, especially with stones and rocks.
Range	Western N America; common in California and Arizona.
Season	Summer.

WHITE-ARMED WOLF SPIDER *Aulonia albimana*

A small, pretty species with a black carapace and grey abdomen vaguely marked with white spots. The legs are dark grey and contrast with the partly white palp which is displayed in signals between the sexes during courtship. The male resembles the female but has black markings on the first pair of legs. The female carries a pure white egg sac attached to the spinnerets. The appearance of this spider makes it unique in the northern hemisphere.

Size   Female to 5 mm; male to 4 mm.
Web   A small sheet with a tubular retreat.
Habitat   Stony or grassy areas and roadsides with a preference for warm, sunny places.
Range   Europe and W Asia, especially in the S.
Season   Adults May–July.

NORTHERN WOLF SPIDER *Arctosa cinerea*

A grey-brown species with a speckled appearance and noticeably banded legs. Its pattern matches the stony background of the riverside habitat. The spider makes a silken burrow beneath stones but is active both day and night. Wolf spiders can be seen at night because their eyes reflect the light of a torch. If covered by rising water, this spider remains in its burrow and breathes from bubbles of air.

Size	Female to 18 mm; male to 13 mm.
Web	None.
Habitat	Stony and sandy riversides and lakesides.
Range	Europe, N America, N Africa, Asia and Japan; in mountains in southern regions.
Season	Adult males April–July; females until September.

Pirate Spider *Pirata piraticus*

A semi-aquatic species which spends much time under water. The carapace is green-brown and marked with a 'V' design. The dark abdomen has a velvety iridescence decorated with purple and white spots. This spider builds a vertical tube in moss; the upper end has an opening from which it darts at passing insects; it can be closed by drawing across a silk veil. The lower end leads into water, where the spider goes if disturbed.

Size Female to 9 mm; male to 6 mm.
Web A small tubular web in moss.
Habitat Marshes, edges of ponds and lakes.
Range Europe and much of Asia to Japan; also N America.
Season Adult males April–July; females all year.

Spotted Wolf Spider *Pardosa amentata*

A small wolf spider with a mottled brown appearance and thin legs. The carapace has a pale central band and the abdomen has a vague series of chevrons. This spider is often active in sunshine. During courtship the male waves his palps up and down; the female vibrates her front legs and adopts a trance-like state. The mother carries the egg sac attached to her spinnerets and, after hatching, the young ride on her back.

Size Female to 8 mm; male to 6 mm.
Web None, and no permanent retreat.
Habitat Open places: grassland, fields, lawns and roadsides.
Range Europe and much of Asia.
Season Adult males April–June; females until August.

WOLF WEAVER *Hippasa foveifera*

One of the minority of wolf spiders which constructs a web. The body and legs are purplish-brown and barred with many narrow pale bands. At the end of the abdomen are two long, flexible spinnerets; the mother attaches her egg sac to them. The male and female are similar in appearance. This spider hides in a silken funnel beside the web and pounces on any grasshopper that lands on it.

Size Female to 12 mm; male to 9 mm.
Web A rough sheet leading to a funnel retreat.
Habitat Forest clearings, grassland and lawns.
Range Central and E Africa.
Season Adults during warm, humid seasons.

NURSERY WEB SPIDER *Pisaura mirabilis*

Known for its unusual method of courtship in which the female requires a present from the male, before mating, of an insect wrapped in silk. Both sexes are grey-brown and a narrow pale stripe runs the length of the carapace and continues as a broad band on the tapering abdomen. The legs are long. The mother carries the huge egg sac under the body, in an awkward 'tiptoe' stance.

Size Female to 15 mm; male to 12 mm.
Web The 'nursery web', a mass of silk, is built around the egg sac to protect the young.
Habitat Woods, meadows, heaths, gardens, roadsides and scrub.
Range Europe, N Africa and much of Asia.
Season Adults June–August.

WEB RUNNER *Euprosthenops australis*

A graceful and impressive, long-legged species. The elongated abdomen has a symmetrical pattern of dark grey and brown. This spider hangs upside down within its tent-like webbing and, if disturbed, disappears with lightning speed into a nearby retreat. The female carries the large spherical egg sac in her jaws under the body and builds a nursery web for the spiderlings.

Size Female to 28 mm; male to 22 mm.
Web A tent-like mass of tough strands within a woody shrub or over a disused animal hole.
Habitat Bushes and low branches of trees.
Range Southern Africa.
Season Adult females probably all year; males October–March.

FALSE WOLF SPIDER *Trechalea* sp.

A long-legged hunting spider resembling the true wolf spiders but with somewhat smaller eyes. The body is olive-brown and the legs, which are curved at the end, are clearly banded. The carapace is circular in outline and is partly overhung by the rather slim abdomen. The spider shown here is a female carrying her brood of up to 100 newly-emerged baby spiderlings on her back, which she does for a number of days.

Size	Female to 20 mm; male unknown.
Web	None.
Habitat	Tropical forest.
Range	Brazil and N Argentina.
Season	Adults probably during warm, humid seasons.

FISHING SPIDER *Dolomedes fimbriatus*

This handsome, dark brown species has a pair of cream or white bands running the length of the body. It is also called the Swamp or Raft Spider, though no raft is made. Rather, this spider hunts by spreading its legs on the water's surface to detect ripples from insects; it also vibrates the legs to attract prey. It can even haul a small fish ashore. After hatching, the young move for a time into waterside bushes and trees.

Size Female to 22 mm; male to 15 mm.
Web None.
Habitat Lakes, ponds, swamps and sluggish streams.
Range Europe and Asia, especially in the S.
Season Adults June–August.

WATER SPIDER *Argyroneta aquatica*

A unique species that lives underwater. It is grey-brown and rather mouse-like. The hairy abdomen is enveloped by a bubble of air when the spider dives below the surface. The jaws are strong (can bite humans) and the male, with longer legs, may be bigger than the female. These spiders eat, mate and lay their eggs in a 'diving-bell', venturing out only to collect air or capture food. The diet includes small fish, tadpoles and other pond life.

Size Female to 15 mm; male to 15 mm.
Web A complex of threads among vegetation underwater. At the centre is the 'diving-bell'.
Habitat Ponds, lakes, dykes and sluggish streams.
Range Europe and much of Asia to Japan.
Season Adults probably all year.

GOLDEN LYNX SPIDER Oxyopes sp.

Lynx spiders are agile hunters which run and jump on low vegetation during the daytime. Golden Lynx Spiders have a domed carapace and a tapered abdomen coloured streaky golden-brown. The legs have numerous spines standing out at right angles. Like other lynx spiders, six of the eight eyes form a hexagon. The female spider guards her egg sac which is attached to a leaf suspended in a mesh of silk threads.

Size Female to 12 mm; male to 10 mm.
Web None, apart from a small nursery web.
Habitat Tropical forest, gardens and scrub.
Range Kenya.
Season Adults probably during warm, humid seasons.

EUROPEAN LYNX SPIDER *Oxyopes lineatus*

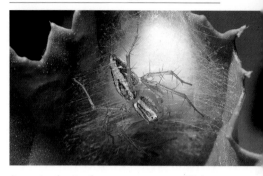

An active daytime hunter on vegetation. With its agility and good vision it springs at small insects and catches them in its spiny legs. The body of the spider is brown; broad pale bands diverge towards the front of both the abdomen and the carapace. During courtship, the male taps the female with his front legs and waves his palps. The female closely guards the egg sac amid a network of silk threads but, unable to hunt, she eventually dies.

Size	Female to 8 mm; male to 7 mm.
Web	None.
Habitat	Trees and bushes in grassland and scrub.
Range	Europe and much of Asia, particularly in the S.
Season	Adults May–September.

AMERICAN GREEN LYNX SPIDER *Peucetia viridans*

A beautiful and athletic green spider with red and black markings in the male. The legs are long and spiny and the abdomen tapers. This spider runs over vegetation with great agility, leaping from stem to stem. The straw-coloured egg sac, which is covered in tubercles and attached firmly to twigs or grass heads, is closely guarded by the mother. A surrounding maze of threads becomes a nursery web for the young when they hatch.

Size Female to 16 mm; male to 13 mm.
Web None, apart from a small nursery web.
Habitat Shrubs and grasses; often in the flowering heads of wild buckwheat.
Range Southern states of USA and Central America.
Season Adults April–August.

African Green Lynx Spider *Peucetia* sp.

An athletic spider coloured a beautiful shade of green. The carapace is grass-green and the abdomen is a mixture of green, yellow and mauve. The long legs are yellow-green with dark bands. These spiders can be seen leaping easily through the leaves of shrubs, either chasing prey or escaping from predators. Their leg span may reach 4 cm and they are said to be able to jump more than 2 cm into the air to seize a flying insect.

Size Female to 15 mm; male unknown.
Web None, apart from a small nursery web.
Habitat Savannah; shrubs and grasses.
Range S Africa.
Season Adults probably October–March.

BUZZING SPIDER *Anyphaena accentuata*

A species which hunts on foliage. The female has a pale grey abdomen with a central marking. The slimmer male (shown here) is darker. During courtship, the male vibrates his abdomen on the surface of a leaf to make a high-pitched buzzing sound, while his front legs are raised upwards. The female builds a tubular silk retreat, often inside the curl of a leaf, in which the eggs are laid during the month of June.

Size	Female to 8 mm; male to 7 mm.
Web	None.
Habitat	Woodland, especially conifers and oak.
Range	Europe and much of Asia.
Season	Adults April–July.

SAC SPIDER *Clubiona reclusa*

A small, pale species with a glossy brown carapace and a silky, grey, elongate abdomen. The jaws are robust and the eyes are in two rows at the front of the carapace. The fourth pair of legs is usually the longest. This spider makes a sac-like retreat in rolled leaves, folded blades of grass, or under loose bark. The retreat is used for egg-laying, moulting and resting, and the spider emerges at night to hunt its small insect prey.

Size Female to 6 mm; male to 4 mm.
Web None.
Habitat On trees and bushes in grassland and woodland.
Range Europe and much of Asia.
Season Adults June–November.

BARK SAC SPIDER *Clubiona corticalis*

A relatively robust sac spider with dark jaws and a glossy brown carapace. The abdomen has a dark central mark which becomes a pattern of chevrons towards the rear. The two sexes are reasonably alike. The species is occasionally found in houses walking across the walls. This spider makes a thick-walled retreat, under stones or loose bark. In this retreat, the mother guards her bundle of yellow eggs.

Size Female to 10 mm; male to 10 mm.
Web None.
Habitat Old trees and buildings.
Range Europe and much of Asia.
Season Adults April–September.

SLENDER SAC SPIDER *Cheiracanthium mildei*

A straw-coloured spider with large, shiny black jaws and a glossy brown carapace. The male is smaller than the female but has longer legs. The flat, papery retreat is built in a folded leaf or, for example, in the folds of curtains. At night the spider leaves the retreat to forage as a hunter. It is fast, agile and quite aggressive. A bite from this species may cause blisters of the skin.

Size	Female to 10 mm; male to 8 mm.
Web	None, but makes a tough, sac-like retreat.
Habitat	Grassland, heather and scrub; buildings in N America.
Range	S Europe, N Africa and W Asia; introduced to N America.
Season	Adults May–July.

VESPA SAC SPIDER *Supunna picta*

A beautifully-marked species that runs about on sunny days, waving its orange first pair of legs in the air and appearing to imitate a solitary hunting wasp waving its antennae. The spider runs very fast in short bursts with frequent changes of direction. The legs and entire body are blue-black with white markings and the front legs are orange. The round egg sac of smooth white silk is flattened against a stone.

Size Female to 7 mm; male to 6 mm.
Web None.
Habitat Eucalypt forest: leaf litter and stones.
Range Eastern Australia.
Season Male and female in summer; egg sac in late autumn.

Arizonan Ground Spider *Castianeira occidens*

A beautifully-marked species with orange-red on the top of the abdomen and a white central band on the black, narrow carapace. The legs are black, becoming reddish towards the ends. These spiders live under stones and logs but they also run rapidly in the open and, by raising their front legs, may resemble large ants. The flattened egg cocoons are usually attached to the underside of a stone.

Size Female to 10 mm; male to 8 mm.
Web None.
Habitat Open, stony ground and pastures.
Range Southwestern N America.
Season Summer.

TRINIDAD ANT SPIDER Myrmecium sp.

A spider that needs double-checking to confirm that it is not an ant. The carapace looks like the separate head and thorax of an ant. The palps of the male spider (shown here) look like an ant's jaws, the front legs are waved like antennae, and the false waist and glossy brown abdomen complete the illusion. The spider lives alongside certain species of ants in order to avoid predation. Only the eight legs give it away!

Size Female unknown; male to 8 mm.
Web None.
Habitat Tropical rainforest.
Range Trinidad.
Season Adults probably all year.

BLACK ANT SPIDER *Aphantochilus sp.*

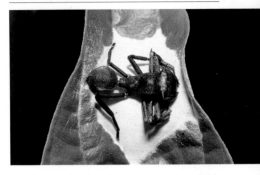

Another species that demonstrates a remarkable imitation of an ant (*Cephalotes* species). This spider is entirely black except for a splash of red at the front of the long, tapering carapace. Either side of the carapace at the front are a pair of horns and the eyes are widely spaced. The short abdomen is rounded, like the ant's. The mother spider guards her eggs in a sac attached firmly to the underside of a leaf.

Size Female to 8 mm; male to 7 mm.
Web None.
Habitat Tropical rainforest.
Range Peru.
Season Unknown.

Glossy Ant Spider *Micaria pulicaria*

A small species with a metallic lustre. The carapace is a glossy brown and the abdomen is an iridescent purple with pale bars across the middle. This spider is active during the day, especially in sunshine, and runs about in an ant-like way, though it is not such a clever mimic as the Trinidad Ant Spider (p.182). The Glossy Ant Spider constructs a silken retreat under a stone, in which the eggs are laid.

Size	Female to 4 mm; male to 3 mm.
Web	None.
Habitat	Open, sunny places in stony heathland and gardens.
Range	Europe and Asia, especially in the S.
Season	Adults June–August.

MOUSE SPIDER *Scotophaeus blackwalli*

This species appears somewhat 'mouse'-like. Both the grey-brown carapace and the grey, furry abdomen are low and flat. In Europe the spider is a nocturnal wanderer on walls where it searches for insect prey. The Mouse Spider does build a web but it spends much time on hunting excursions. Very occasionally, this species bites, but this is unlikely to be serious.

Size	Female to 12 mm; male to 10 mm.
Web	Generally none, but occasionally builds a loose sheet.
Habitat	Buildings; holes in walls and under loose tree bark.
Range	Europe, Asia and N America.
Season	Adult females all year; males spring–autumn.

WHITE-TAILED SPIDER *Lampona cylindrata*

A sleek, furry spider with a rather slender and cylindrical body. The colour ranges from grey to reddish-brown or bluish-black but there is always a white spot at the end of the abdomen. The male has a hard plate towards the front of the abdomen. At night this vagabond spider forages on walls, walking slowly and deliberately; it may enter the webs of other spiders and capture the host. It can bite humans and the effects are felt around the bite.

Size Female to 14 mm; male to 10 mm.
Web None.
Habitat On trees and buildings.
Range S Australia and Tasmania; introduced to New Zealand.
Season Both sexes mature in late summer.

STONE SPIDER *Drassodes lapidosus*

A robust, dull-coloured species with a low, silky-brown carapace, dark jaws and a grey, elongate abdomen. The legs are reddish-brown and two of the eight eyes are silvery. This spider is a nocturnal hunter which spends the day in a sac or tube-like retreat under stones or loose bark. Its insect prey is swathed with a broad band of silk before being bitten. The female lays her eggs inside the retreat.

Size Female to 18 mm; male to 12 mm.
Web None, but the retreat has strong, sheet-like webbing.
Habitat Under stones, leaf litter and other debris.
Range Europe, N Africa and much of Asia to Japan.
Season Adult females probably all year; males April–November.

BLACK ZIPPER *Zelotes apricorum*

A nocturnal hunter which rests during the day in a retreat under stones and leaf litter. Most of the body, and the legs, has a sleek, black appearance. The abdomen is fairly elongate and the carapace narrows noticeably at the front. The male is similar but even slimmer. The egg sacs are papery and fixed to the bottom of a stone; they are guarded by the female though she runs off at high speed if disturbed.

Size Female to 9 mm; male to 6 mm.
Web None.
Habitat Grassland, heathland and woodland.
Range Europe and much of Asia.
Season Adults May–July.

BANDED CRAWLER *Poecilocroa conspicua*

An attractively-marked hunting spider which, though it has retiring habits, is active both day and night. The carapace is a glossy grey-black and the abdomen is a furry black with two white bands, the last divided. The legs are black and brown. The male and female are similar in appearance. This spider constructs a silken retreat under a stone in which the eggs are laid.

Size Female to 8 mm; male to 7 mm.
Web None.
Habitat On trees and stony ground in grassland, woodland and scrub.
Range S Europe and W Asia.
Season Adults May–July.

SAND SPIDER *Pterotricha simoni*

A slender, sandy-coloured species with rather long legs and long, prominent spinnerets. Because of its appearance, this spider is well camouflaged in its sandy habitat. The male and female are reasonably similar in appearance. The long, flexible spinnerets enable the spider to effectively truss up a victim in silk as the spider rapidly encircles it. It preys on insects of sandy habitats.

Size Female to 12 mm; male to 10 mm.
Web None.
Habitat Under cover of stones and shrubs in dry, sandy areas.
Range Spain and Portugal.
Season Adults November–May.

BRAZILIAN WANDERING SPIDER *Phoneutria nigriventer*

A notorious species which causes considerable fear. This spider is large, fast, agile and bites readily. When provoked, it makes a threat display by raising the first two pairs of legs and exposing the red jaws. Most of the body is sandy-brown but the underside reveals a patch of black. The legs are strong and spiny. The spider hunts large insects and small vertebrates. Egg cocoons are deposited under stones, loose tree bark and leaves.

Size Female to 35 mm; male to 25 mm.
Web None.
Habitat Buildings, plantations and wasteland; in banana leaves, etc.
Range S Brazil and Paraguay.
Season Adults all year.

191

KENYAN HUNTING SPIDER *Ctenus* sp.

A large grey and silver, long-legged spider which resembles the wolf spiders (pp.158–166). Like other species of the genus, this one is a vagrant which builds no retreat but rests inside spiny and prickly plants. On the spider's abdomen, tufts of stiff white hairs may be seen projecting upwards. The female carries her enormous egg sac under her body. This spider is likely to be aggressive if provoked and may give a painful bite.

Size Female to 25 mm; male to 20 mm.
Web None.
Habitat Tropical forest and savannah.
Range Kenya.
Season Adults probably all year.

Rusty Wandering Spider *Cupiennius getazi*

A beautiful, rust-coloured and fast-moving spider. The entire body, including the long legs, is orange-brown, but a darker brown band runs from the front of the carapace to the end of the abdomen. At the front of the abdomen this band encloses a silvery wedge and towards the rear it breaks up into crescent bars. The spider's hunting tactics are to lie quietly in ambush and then launch a rapid attack on prey that comes close.

Size Female to 30 mm; male to 22 mm.
Web None.
Habitat Tropical forest.
Range Central America: Panama and Costa Rica.
Season Adults probably all year.

HUNTSMAN SPIDER *Heteropoda venatoria*

A familiar spider in SE Asia and the Caribbean where it is welcomed because it eats cockroaches. It emerges at night from its hiding place to wander over walls. It is brown and the oval carapace has two cream bands, one at the back and one under the two rows of eyes. The legs are extended sideways. The female holds her large, cushion-shaped egg sac under the body.

Size Female to 30 mm; male to 22 mm.
Web None.
Habitat Buildings, banana plantations, secondary forest and rocks.
Range Cosmopolitan in tropics and subtropics.
Season Adults all year.

GIANT CRAB SPIDER *Eusparassus dufouri*

A pale, grey-brown, leggy species with a pattern of chevrons on the abdomen and a large black patch underneath. The legs extend sideways like a crab's, and are clearly banded. This spider constructs a tough, papery silken sac which it sticks firmly to the underside of a stone. The sac is used for resting, moulting and egg-laying. If opened, the spider dashes out and runs to the other side of the stone.

Size	Female to 20 mm; male to 15 mm.
Web	None.
Habitat	Stony areas, dry river beds and walls of old buildings.
Range	S Europe and N Africa.
Season	Adult females all year; adult males March–June.

195

MEADOW SPIDER *Micrommata virescens*

This hunter is one of the relatively few green spiders. The female has a green carapace and legs and a lemon-green abdomen with a darker cardiac mark. The male is especially beautiful with a red and yellow striped abdomen, which blends well with the flowering heads of grass. These spiders wait head-down, ready to spring on passing insects. A retreat is built by silking together leaves near the ground.

Size Female to 15 mm; male to 10 mm.
Web None.
Habitat Grassland and woodland glades.
Range Europe and much of Asia to Japan.
Season Adults April–July.

GIANT HUNTSMAN *Holconia immanis*

An impressive species, especially when found in a house. The carapace is dark olive-brown and the abdomen pale grey with a black cardiac mark. The long banded legs extend sideways. This spider is an agile, nocturnal hunter whose diet includes large insects and small vertebrates. During the mating season, the male and female cohabit. The female guards her eggs and cares for the young. The spider's bite is painful but not highly toxic.

Size	Female to 35 mm; male to 25 mm.
Web	None.
Habitat	Forest, gardens and in buildings.
Range	Australia; introduced to New Zealand.
Season	Adult females all year; males October–April.

MALAYSIAN HUNTSMAN *Isopeda* sp.

A handsome, long-legged species active mostly at night. The general coloration is olive-brown but is paler on top with a darker band in the middle of the carapace. The body and especially the banded legs have a thick covering of hairs. The sexes are similar in appearance. The female (shown here) stands guard to defend her nest which is made out of two large leaves stuck together with silk.

Size	Female to 32 mm; male to 25 mm.
Web	None.
Habitat	Tropical rainforest.
Range	Malaysia.
Season	Adults probably all year.

LICHEN HUNTSMAN *Pandercetes gracilis*

Beautifully camouflaged on mossy, lichen-covered tree trunks, this spider is very difficult to see. If approached too closely, it moves at great speed to the other side of the tree. The hairiness of the legs and body, pressed close against the bark, helps to hide the spider's outline and reduce shadows. The male and female are similar in appearance. The egg sac is attached to the bark and the female stands guard above it.

Size	Female to 20 mm; male to 15 mm.
Web	None.
Habitat	Trees in tropical forest.
Range	Australia (NE Queensland) and New Guinea.
Season	Adults probably all year.

FOREST HUNTSMAN *Pandercetes plumipes*

Another camouflaged species that blends well with mossy, lichen-covered tree trunks. The hairiness of the legs and body, pressed close against the tree, helps to hide the spider's outline and shadow. The eight eyes are grouped in a raised region at the front of the carapace. The male and female are similar in appearance. The mother spider stands guard over the flattened egg sac which is attached to the bark.

Size	Female to 20 mm; male to 15 mm.
Web	None.
Habitat	Tropical rainforest and gardens.
Range	Malaysia.
Season	Adults probably all year.

Wall Crab Spider *Selenops radiatus*

A mottled-brown, fast-moving hunting spider with banded legs. Holding its legs out to the sides, this species is distinctly crab-like but is best recognised by its extreme flatness; in some countries they are called 'flatties'. The cryptic coloration makes them almost invisible on trees and rocks but they are obvious on a plain wall. They sit face down without moving but if disturbed dash sideways into a crevice or behind a picture.

Size	Female to 15 mm; male to 12 mm.
Web	None.
Habitat	Buildings, plantations, rocks and tree trunks.
Range	Widespread in tropical and subtropical regions, including S Spain.
Season	Adults all year.

Two-Tailed Spider *Hersilia bicornutus*

In the resting, head-down position, the flattened, lichen-coloured body of this spider casts no shadow and is difficult to see on a tree trunk. When it moves, it is extremely quick and will rapidly encircle an insect, wrapping it with silk from two very long spinnerets resembling tails. The abdomen is flat and wider behind than in front. The legs are long and the front of the oval carapace has a mound which carries the eyes in a compact group.

Size	Female to 12 mm; male to 10 mm.
Web	Nothing significant.
Habitat	Stony scrubland, stone walls and tree trunks.
Range	S Europe and N Africa.
Season	Adults March–July.

CRAB SPIDERS

Crab spiders do not spin webs. They are characterised by having the first two pairs of legs longer and stronger than the last two pairs. The legs tend to be held out to the sides and the eight small eyes are often widely spaced. Though mostly small, many are believed to have venom which has a potent effect on insects.

In the family Thomisidae, the hunting tactics are sedentary and based on camouflage and ambushing prey. Males are often much smaller than females and quite different in appearance. In the family Philodromidae, where the sexes are relatively similar, prey is usually caught by speed as in many other hunting spiders.

WANDERING CRAB SPIDER *Philodromus aureolus*

A fast-running hunter on trees and bushes. The rich brown carapace of the female has a broad pale central band and the slightly flattened, paler abdomen has chevrons with a cardiac mark. The male has a broad carapace and is generally darker brown with a metallic lustre. In both sexes, the crab-like legs are of similar length. The mother attaches her egg sacs to leaves or bark.

Size	Female to 6 mm; male to 4 mm.
Web	None.
Habitat	Woodland, heathland and gardens; on leaves and tree trunks.
Range	Europe, Asia, Japan and N America.
Season	Adults April–July.

HOUSE CRAB SPIDER *Philodromus dispar*

An active hunter which can move forwards, backwards or sideways. In common with other crab spiders, the legs extend sideways. The female's carapace has a pale band along the centre but the buff-coloured abdomen has only a vague pattern. The male (shown here) is quite distinctive with both carapace and abdomen appearing iridescent blue-black. The legs are brown. *Philodromus* has eight eyes arranged in two curved rows.

Size	Female to 6 mm; male to 4 mm.
Web	None.
Habitat	Old trees and buildings.
Range	Europe, much of Asia, and N America.
Season	Adults April–July.

LICHEN CRAB SPIDER *Philodromus margaritatus*

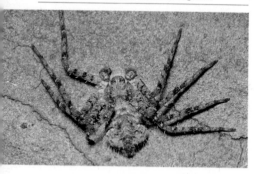

A beautifully-camouflaged species which is difficult to see on lichen-covered bark and tree foliage. The long legs, carapace and abdomen of the female are pale whitish-green with variable degrees of black markings. The very long-legged male is darker, especially on the carapace. This spider waits in ambush for passing insects and moves rapidly to attack. The jaws are small, like those of other crab spiders, and the prey is sucked dry rather than mashed up.

Size Female to 8 mm; male to 5 mm.
Web None.
Habitat Old-growth forest and woodland.
Range Europe and much of Asia to Japan.
Season Adults April–July.

DIAMOND SPIDER *Thanatus formicinus*

A prettily-marked, free-living hunter. The female is brown with a broad, pale buff band on the carapace and a pale buff abdomen with a long, dark, diamond cardiac mark. The male is similar but yet more handsome; the brown is replaced by black, including on the legs. The Diamond Spider lives on grasses and tree trunks and its diet includes moths found in the crevices of bark.

Size	Female to 12 mm; male to 7 mm.
Web	None.
Habitat	Grassland, heathland and scrub.
Range	Europe, N America and much of Asia.
Season	Adults April–July.

GRASS SPIDER *Tibellus oblongus*

A striped, long-bodied hunting spider at home among tall grass and reed stems. The female is straw-coloured but the body also has a dark band along the entire length. The male is similar but the abdomen is bluish-grey. When resting, the spider stretches out inconspicuously along a twig or grass stem. Unless it moves, it is difficult to see. The female attaches her egg sac near the top of grasses and stands guard over it.

Size Female to 12 mm; male to 9 mm.
Web None.
Habitat Grassy, shrubby places.
Range Europe, much of Asia, Japan and N America.
Season Adults April–July.

HEATHER SPIDER *Thomisus onustus*

This spider may be pink, yellow or white, depending on the colour of the flower on which it is found. In heather, for example, it is pink. Like other crab spiders that ambush their prey, the first two pairs of legs, used for grasping insects, are longer and stronger than the last two. The female has a broad, angular abdomen and the carapace has two horn-like projections near the eyes. The smaller male is orange-brown with blackish legs.

Size Female to 8 mm; male to 5 mm.
Web None.
Habitat Heathers and other flowers in heathland, meadows and edges of cultivation.
Range Europe, N Africa, Asia and Japan.
Season Adults April–July.

WHITE CRAB SPIDER *Thomisus spectabilis*

A handsome crab spider. The legs and carapace are translucent white, while the angular abdomen is pure white with a black spot at each corner. Sometimes the overall colour is yellow or pink. The little brown male is so different he seems to be unrelated. The strong front legs of·the female are held open to catch large and small insects, including green tree ants. The egg sac is usually concealed in a leaf folded with tough white silk.

Size	Female to 12 mm; male to 3 mm.
Web	None.
Habitat	Tropical forest edges and gardens.
Range	SE Asia from India to Queensland.
Season	Adult females probably all year; males during warm, humid seasons.

COMMON CRAB SPIDER *Xysticus cristatus*

A typical but secretive crab spider. The carapace of the female has a broad pale band enclosing a triangular mark and the abdomen is marked with a pattern of chevrons. Like many other crab spiders, this species ambushes its prey, grabbing them with strong front legs. The small male is relatively dark. During courtship the male wraps the female loosely with silk. The mother spider builds a brood chamber among undergrowth.

Size	Female to 8 mm; male to 5 mm.
Web	None.
Habitat	Undergrowth in grassland and woodland.
Range	Europe, N Africa and much of Asia; common generally.
Season	Adults April–July.

FLOWER SPIDER *Misumena vatia*

Any innocent flower can conceal this crab spider which waits to ambush a visiting insect. The female spider may be white, green or yellow; its colour can change slowly to blend with the shade of the flower, though sometimes the abdomen may be striped with red. The small but lanky male has a brown carapace and legs with a buff-coloured abdomen. The female spider is a formidable predator and will attack insects much larger than itself.

Size Female to 10 mm; male to 5 mm.
Web None.
Habitat Flowery places; meadows and gardens.
Range Europe, N Africa, Asia, Japan and N America.
Season Adults April–July.

GREEN CRAB SPIDER *Diaea dorsata*

A pretty species in which the female's carapace and legs are entirely green, while the abdomen is covered in a wide brown pattern. This coloration gives camouflage on plants where the spider waits to ambush insects. The male is mostly brown with pale green legs. There is no permanent retreat but the female makes a flimsy silk shelter to enclose the woolly egg cocoons. She usually guards her eggs until they hatch.

Size   Female to 6 mm; male to 4 mm.
Web   None.
Habitat   Woodland and gardens, usually on trees, bushes and shrubs.
Range   Europe and much of Asia.
Season   Adults April–July.

213

Strawberry and Cream Spider *Diaea* sp.

A beautiful spider with translucent white legs and carapace. A bold pattern of 'strawberry jam' occupies much of the yellow and cream-coloured abdomen, which has a rhomboidal shape. The appearance of this spider is probably intended to give it camouflage inside a flower. Like other similar species, this crab spider has long front legs, which it extends in 'open-armed' fashion, and shorter rear legs, with which it holds on to the plant.

Size   Female approx. 6 mm; male unknown.
Web   None.
Habitat   Tropical rainforest.
Range   New Guinea.
Season   Little known.

BIRD-DROPPING SPIDER *Phrynarachne rugosa*

A bizarre species that, at rest, resembles a bird's dropping. The blobs and warts all over the black-and-white glazed surface give the spider a wet and lumpy look. It draws its legs in and waits motionless on a leaf for hours. Sometimes it adds to the deception by sitting beside a small, messy-looking patch of white silk. Also, cunningly, the spider emits a smell to attract flies which are lured straight to its grasping legs.

Size	Female to 10 mm; male to 6 mm.
Web	None.
Habitat	Tropical forest and undergrowth.
Range	Sub-Saharan Africa and Madagascar.
Season	Adults probably all year.

SIX-SPOT CRAB SPIDER _Platythomisus sexmaculatus_

A large, strikingly-marked species. It is an unusual kind of crab spider, and little is known of its biology. The carapace is orange-brown with a black band running through the eyes. The legs are orange-brown becoming black at the knees. The long, oval abdomen is orange and white on top with six large black patches followed by three smaller patches.

Size Female to 15 mm; male unknown.
Web Builds a rudimentary web on a leaf.
Habitat Tropical forest and savannah, especially beside rivers.
Range N Africa.
Season Adults probably during rainy seasons.

GOLD LEAF CRAB SPIDER *Synema globosum*

A small, rounded, web-less spider common in the Mediterranean where it may be seen scuttling around open flowers. The glossy abdomen of the female is black with a strongly-indented pattern of yellow, gold or red. The carapace is black but around the eyes is pale brown. The legs are brown or black and the front two pairs are darkest. The male is black with a white bar on the abdomen.

Size Female to 6 mm; male to 4 mm.
Web None.
Habitat Flowering plants such as umbellifers, in woodland and open areas.
Range S and Central Europe, N Africa and S Asia to Japan.
Season Adults April–July.

217

SEVEN-SPINED CRAB SPIDER *Epicadus heterogaster*

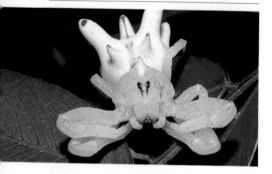

A curious but beautiful species which appears to imitate a white, orchid-like flower. Insects which visit the 'flower' to sample its nectar unexpectedly find themselves in the deadly embrace of the spider. The female's spiny carapace and strong legs are translucent white. The pearly-white abdomen has seven huge, black-tipped spines and a yellow band. The small male is similar but it is red-brown with white markings.

Size Female to 12 mm; male to 5 mm.
Web None.
Habitat Tropical forest.
Range S America, from Venezuela to N Argentina.
Season Adults probably during warm, humid seasons.

KNOBBLY CRAB SPIDER *Stephanopis altifrons*

A large crab spider with an angular abdomen ornamented with spiny and knobbly tubercles. This rugged shape, together with the spider's habit of sitting with legs folded tightly to the body, makes it difficult to detect on a tree trunk, even at a distance of only a few centimetres, unless it moves. During the night, the spider roams over the bark looking for insects. The egg sac, placed in a crevice, is camouflaged with particles of tree bark.

Size	Female to 12 mm; male to 10 mm.
Web	None.
Habitat	Tree bark in eucalypt forest and Acacia thickets.
Range	Australia (eastern states).
Season	Adults November–March.

JUMPING SPIDERS

Jumping spiders are alert, mobile hunters with good eyesight. Their eight eyes are widely spaced, with two large ones at the front. Jumpers are mostly small and their bright colours are displayed during courtship. They rarely spin webs. They usually stalk their victim until close enough to jump. The power for jumping comes from the last two pairs of legs.

The large number of jumping spiders in the world (about 4000 species) belongs to a single family, the Salticidae. Jumping spiders are most abundant in tropical countries and become scarce towards the Poles. Some of the most spectacular belong to the genus *Phidippus* of North America.

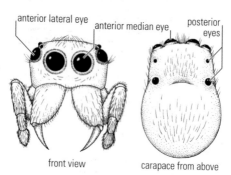

anterior lateral eye   anterior median eye   posterior eyes

front view   carapace from above

ZEBRA SPIDER *Salticus scenicus*

A jumping spider that stalks insects on walls and never falls off! Like other jumping spiders, it launches itself with the four back legs after first fixing a safety line to the substrate. It also has excellent vision; the two large front eyes can identify prey. The Zebra Spider's carapace is glossy black and the abdomen is black or brown with three white bands. The male has a huge pair of jaws to restrain the female during mating.

Size Female to 7 mm; male to 5 mm.
Web None.
Habitat Walls, buildings, rocks and trees.
Range Europe, much of Asia and N America.
Season Adults April–August.

GRASS JUMPER *Evarcha flammata*

A handsome little species with a lustrous carapace and a dark, velvety-brown abdomen. Like other jumping spiders, the eight eyes are in three rows. The male (shown here) is recognised by the white 'face' and the large first pair of legs adorned with tufts of white hairs. During courtship, the two sexes signal to each other with movements of their legs and palps. These spiders construct a nest in dead grasses and other plants.

Size Female to 7 mm; male to 5 mm.
Web None.
Habitat Grassland and heathland.
Range Europe, Asia and N America.
Season Adults April–July.

SUNSHINE JUMPER *Heliophanus flavipes*

A small jumping spider with an iridescent purple-black body, plus some white markings on the abdomen. The palps and legs are yellow in the female with some black streaks on the legs; the male's legs are generally darker. Like other jumping spiders, this species has a sac-like nest made of a thick white sheet. Such sacs are constructed in a great variety of places, for example in rolled-up leaves, under rocks or in the empty shells of snails.

Size	Female to 6 mm; male to 4 mm.
Web	None.
Habitat	Grassland and heathland.
Range	Europe and much of Asia.
Season	Adults April–July.

FENCE-POST JUMPER *Marpissa muscosa*

A jumping spider whose habits match its appearance. The camouflaged body is flat so that it can rest beneath the peeling bark of fence posts or under stones. The female's carapace is dark, lustrous brown and the abdomen is grey-brown with a pattern of chevrons. The male is similar but darker. In both sexes, the first pair of legs are the heaviest and the palps are hairy. This spider often emerges to hunt in the late afternoon.

Size Female to 10 mm; male to 8 mm.
Web None.
Habitat Woodland edges, trees, hedges, fence posts and stone walls; occasionally in buildings.
Range Europe and much of Asia.
Season Adults April–July.

PANTROPICAL JUMPER *Plexippus paykulli*

A common jumping spider in warm countries. The female has a pale central band or series of pale marks on the dark abdomen, and the dark carapace has a pale patch in the middle. The male is more strongly marked with a white central band or series of spots along the body. Like most jumping spiders, the carapace is rectangular and, in the male, as large as the abdomen.

Size Female to 12 mm; male to 10 mm.
Web None.
Habitat Woodland, plantations, gardens, rocks and buildings.
Range Cosmopolitan in tropical and subtropical regions, including Japan and southern USA.
Season Adults may occur all year in many places.

225

MOSQUITO CATCHER *Hasarius adansoni*

A smaller species than the previous one, this jumping spider is also common around houses in warm countries. The female has a black carapace and an olive abdomen with a brown central band. The male has a white semicircle on the back of the carapace. This species has been introduced many times to Europe and N America along with exotic plants but in cold climates it only seems to survive in hot houses.

Size	Female to 8 mm; male to 6 mm.
Web	None.
Habitat	Buildings, walls, plantations, gardens; often on plants.
Range	Cosmopolitan in tropics and subtropics.
Season	Adults probably all year.

BEAUTIFUL JUMPER *Philaeus chrysops*

This southern species has a striking appearance. The female's carapace is black and the abdomen and front legs are orange-red. The carapace of the male (shown here) is black and the red abdomen has a black band. The male's legs are orange at the front and white at the back. The bright colours are displayed in courtship as the two sexes dance and wave their legs and palps. The mother spider hides with her eggs in a silken nest in a crevice.

Size Female to 12 mm; male to 8 mm.
Web None.
Habitat Woodland, heathland, rocks and scrub.
Range S Europe, N Africa and W Asia.
Season Adults April–July.

AUDACIOUS JUMPER Phidippus audax

An impressive jumping spider that commands attention by its size and alertness. The female is black with white bands on the carapace, and one large and two smaller white spots on the abdomen. The handsome male is black with white bands and plumes of hairs on the legs. Both sexes have robust, hairy front legs and iridescent green jaws. The female spider makes a small nursery web to take care of the young.

Size Female to 15 mm; male to 13 mm.
Web None apart from a web for the young.
Habitat Woodland and gardens; tree trunks, shrubs and stones.
Range N America; the largest specimens occur in the S.
Season Adults probably April–September.

APACHE JUMPER *Phidippus insolens*

An eye-catching spider with almost human qualities of alertness. Like others of the genus, this species is highly sensitive to the presence of humans and usually rapidly runs away. The male (shown here) is almost entirely orange-red apart from the black, hairy legs and palps. To a degree, the male resembles certain velvet ants. The female is less colourful, with a dark brown abdomen marked by a variable red pattern.

Size	Female to 12 mm; male to 9 mm.
Web	None.
Habitat	Upland shrubs and flowery grassland.
Range	N America: Rocky Mountain states.
Season	Adults probably April–August.

DANDY JUMPER *Portia schultzi*

A peculiar jumping spider with a strange, hesitant way of walking. Often, the spider just resembles a piece of debris because of its posture and the ornate tufts of hair on the body and thin legs. The female is distinguished by a band of white hairs above the jaws. This spider is sharp-eyed and highly adept at catching insects and even other jumping spiders. The male (shown here) often drums its cream-coloured palps in an excited manner.

Size Female to 10 mm; male to 8 mm.
Web Occasionally builds a small sheet-web as a refuge.
Habitat Tropical forest.
Range E and S Africa.
Season Adults during warm, humid seasons.

TREE JUMPER *Phaeacius* sp.

A jumping spider which uses sit-and-wait tactics. The entire body and legs are a combination of grey and white; the flanks are grey and the wide central band is grey-white. This spider's low profile and general hairiness make it difficult to see on a tree trunk unless it moves. Like other jumping spiders, it takes care to fix a line to the tree before it jumps – so that if it misses its prey, it can haul itself back up the line.

Size	Female to 12 mm; male to 9 mm.
Web	None.
Habitat	Tropical rainforest.
Range	Sri Lanka.
Season	Adults probably most of the year.

HEAVY JUMPER *Hyllus giganteus*

A thickset, furry-looking spider which jumps impressively from leaf to leaf. The abdomen is dark brown with a pattern of pale, striped markings. The carapace is also dark brown. The legs and much of the body are densely covered in hairs, especially the palps. Like other jumping spiders, four eyes at the front look forward, and four on top look up and to the sides. The two large central front eyes recognise prey at a distance.

Size Female to 15 mm; male to 10 mm.
Web None.
Habitat Forest edges, mangroves and shrubby places.
Range Indonesia and N Australia.
Season Adults probably most of the year.

WOOLLY-LEGGED JUMPER *Saitis barbipes*

A small, charming spider. The male (shown here) is very pretty: he has a brown body, with grey on top and orange at the front of the carapace. The gaudy, hairy, third pair of legs is larger than the others. They are orange with a black and white tip. During courtship they are displayed by being raised up and outwards. The female is pale brown with a spotted abdomen.

Size Female to 6 mm; male to 5 mm.
Web None.
Habitat In undergrowth and leaf litter of woods and heaths.
Range Europe; most common in S.
Season Adults April–July.

BACK-TO-FRONT JUMPER *Orsima ichneumon*

This species has a rear end that looks like the front end of a small wasp. The spider's spinnerets imitate the antennae of the insect and the brown-patterned abdomen is shaped to look like its head and thorax. The last two legs are dark but the other six are pale and they combine with the green carapace to suggest wings. By misleading predators, this spider has a greater chance of escape. It can also retreat in an unexpected direction.

Size Female to 6 mm; male to 5 mm.
Web None.
Habitat Tropical rainforest.
Range Malaysia and Indonesia (Borneo, Sumatra and Malay Peninsula).
Season Adults probably all year.

SPEAR-JAWED JUMPER *Myrmarachne plataleoides*

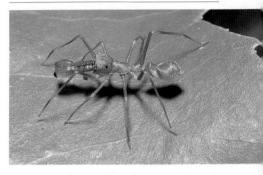

An ant-mimicking spider with an impressive pair of jaws, particularly in the male. The body is long and constricted to increase its resemblance to ants. The spider usually occurs on trees and shrubs which are inhabited by red ants but probably does not feed on them. The purpose of the mimicry is to fool predators who avoid ants. The spiders are very careful to avoid being attacked by the ants, which are not fooled by the mimicry.

Size	Female to 8 mm; male to 10 mm (including jaws).
Web	None.
Habitat	Tropical forest and shrubby mountainsides.
Range	S Asia: India and Nepal to Malaysia.
Season	Adults during warm, humid seasons.

LEAF JUMPER *Lysommanes viridis*

An elegant, athletic species which is at home on the leaves of forest trees. The beautiful green carapace and green legs are similar in both sexes; the abdomen is a little more brown. At the front of the carapace is a strongly-marked brown and white region enclosing the eyes. The eight eyes are arranged in four rows of two. The two largest, at the front, focus on the insect prey after the other eyes have detected its movement.

Size Female to 12 mm; male to 10 mm.
Web None.
Habitat Forest, gardens and shrubby land.
Range Southeastern USA, Central America and the Caribbean.
Season Adults during warm, humid seasons.

PAINTER'S JUMPER *Mopsus mormon*

A fine spider with excellent camouflage on leaves. In the female almost the entire body is green except for the white-ringed eyes surrounded by red and white markings. The handsome male has black and white whiskers, a green carapace, a red eye region high above the black jaws and a light green abdomen with two narrow black stripes. The female makes a brood chamber for the young. The diet includes various insects.

  Size Female to 15 mm; male to 12 mm.
  Web None.
  Habitat Tropical forest, grass and heathland; on leaves.
  Range Eastern Australia, New Guinea and Solomon Islands.
  Season Adults November–March (Australia).

AUSSIE JUMPER *Helpis minitabunda*

A slim, elegant jumping spider. In the male, the entire body is an iridescent brown, relatively pale on top. The legs are dark with some pale banding. The female is generally less dark. Like many other jumping spiders, the males fight rival males at mating time. The male shown here is standing on a veil of silk, across a leaf, built by the female to create a shelter.

Size Female to 6 mm; male to 5 mm.
Web None.
Habitat Eucalypt forest and shrubby grassland.
Range Eastern Australia and New Zealand.
Season Adults probably during the summer.

BLACK SPOTTED JUMPER Acragus sp.

A jumping spider strikingly marked with orange and black, a combination of colours which gives a warning to other creatures. This spider's coloration is probably intended to mimic a distasteful insect (probably a kind of wasp) which predators should avoid. The problem for spiders in general is that they are good to eat so they have many predators such as birds, lizards, mammals and other spiders.

Size	Female to 10 mm; male to 8 mm.
Web	None.
Habitat	Tropical rainforest.
Range	Brazil and Argentina.
Season	Adults probably all year.

BURROWING SCORPION *Opisthopthalmus carinatus*

This S African species is one of the heavily-built scorpions that uses large, lobster-like pincers to grab prey. It has pale pincers, yellow legs and a yellow sting at the end of a slender tail. The venom is less toxic than that of many other scorpions with weaker pincers. Scorpions are an ancient form of life that has existed for about 400 million years and are notable for the fact that the young are born alive and carried on the mother's back.

Size	Male and female to 10 cm.
Web	None.
Habitat	Savannah and veld; makes a burrow in hard soil.
Range	S Africa.
Season	Present all year but most active during summer.

EUROPEAN HARVESTMAN *Leiobunum rotundum*

Harvestmen are so called because they are numerous at harvest-time. This species, like the others, has no venom or silk glands. Its extremely long legs are used to detect and encircle small insects. The grey-brown body is in one piece and the two eyes sit back to back on a small tubercle. The female's body is larger than the male's. Unlike in spiders, there is little or no courtship before mating and the eggs are laid in the soil.

Size Female to 7 mm; male to 4 mm (length of second leg up to 5 cm).
Web None.
Habitat Woods, fields and hedgerows.
Range Europe.
Season June–November.

241

AMERICAN WHIP SCORPION *Mastigoproctus giganteus*

This species is one of the largest of the whip scorpions. These nocturnal creatures, which are not as fierce as they look, are also known as vinegaroons because they defend themselves with a spray of acetic acid (vinegar). Whip scorpions have heavily-armed pedipalps but no poisonous bite or sting. The long, whip-like tail is used only for detecting environmental conditions.

Size   Female to 65 mm; male to 55 mm (10 cm including appendages).

Web   None.

Habitat   Dry and wooded country, living in burrows and under stones.

Range   Southern states of USA and Mexico.

Season   Present all year; most active during summer.

AFRICAN WHIP SPIDER *Damon variegatus*

Whip spiders, like the whip scorpions (opposite), are bizarre-looking but harmless creatures. They lack a tail but have long, spiny pedipalps with which they grasp insects. The very long, whip-like, first pair of legs are not used for walking but for sensing prey at a distance; for example, further away on a wall. This species has a mottled appearance with banded legs (alternately light and dark).

Size Female to 35 mm; male to 30 mm.
Web None.
Habitat Caves, mines and between rocks; also in disused dwellings.
Range E Africa from Ethiopia to the Cape.
Season Present all year; breeding during rainy seasons.

AFRICAN CAMEL SPIDER *Solpuga* sp.

Camel spiders are also known as sun spiders, wind scorpions and solifugids. They are fast-running creatures with huge, forward-projecting jaws and are said to be able to kill camels – a complete myth. There is a large number of species of camel spiders worldwide: most inhabit hot, dry regions and usually hunt insect prey at night. Their slender legs are generally long and are furnished with many erect hairs – when running they can resemble a ball of fluff.

Size	Female to 40 mm; male to 30 mm.
Web	None.
Habitat	Dry, sandy or stony country.
Range	S Africa.
Season	Most active during summer.

PSEUDOSCORPION Cordylochernes sp.

Pseudoscorpions resemble tiny scorpions but they lack a tail and have no sting. They are so small that they are rarely seen but are in fact quite common, and there is a large number of species worldwide. They are noticed most often when attached to an insect such as a fly or beetle. This 'hitching a lift' is known as phoresy and many do it to reach new places. The pseudoscorpion shown here is holding on to the back of a harlequin beetle.

Size	Female and male to 2.5 mm.
Web	None.
Habitat	Forest leaf litter.
Range	S and Central America.
Season	Unknown.

HARD TICK *Amblyomma sp.*

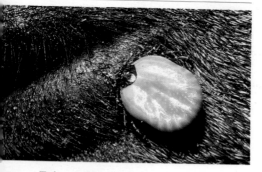

Ticks are strange relatives of spiders which are parasitic instead of predatory. They attach firmly to the skin and suck the blood of animals and humans. Hard ticks have three meals in their lifetime; a single meal can increase their weight as much as 100 times. Soft ticks differ from hard ticks in that they feed little and often. Shown here is a female hard tick attached to the eye of a tapir; the tick is about halfway to becoming fully engorged.

Size	Female to 6 mm (20 mm fully fed); male to 4 mm.
Web	None.
Habitat	Rainforest.
Range	S America.
Season	Active in warm, humid seasons.

SPIDER MITE *Tetranychus* sp.

Mites are minute relatives of spiders. They often exist in huge numbers. Spider mites are one of the groups of mites which are known for their ability to produce silk (from their mouthparts). They feed on plants and crops and are serious pests. They often invade houses in summer and at times can be seen whizzing around on stonework. Usually they are red or orange.

Size	Female and male about 0.5 mm.
Web	A mass of webbing among the leaves of plants.
Habitat	Agricultural land, plantations, gardens, heathland and woods.
Range	Worldwide.
Season	Summer and autumn.

FURTHER READING

The list begins with introductory books and ends with more specialised works.

Hillyard, P. (1994) **The Book of the Spider** From Arachnophobia to the Love of Spiders. Pimlico.

Chinery, M. (1993) **Spiders.** Whittet Books.

Murphy, F. (1980) **Keeping Spiders, Insects and other Land Invertebrates**. Bartholomew.

Baxter, R. (1993) **Keeping and Breeding Tarantulas**. Chudleigh.

Preston-Mapham, R. (1991) **Spiders** An Illustrated Guide. Quarto.

Simon-Brunet, B. (1994) **The Silken Web** A Natural History of Australian Spiders. Reed Books.

Roberts, M. J. (1995) **Collins Field Guide to Spiders of Britain and Northern Europe.** HarperCollins.

Locket, G. H. & Millidge, A. F. **British Spiders** vols 1 & 2 1951/3 (reprinted 1975) & vol 3 (with Merrett, P. 1974). Ray Society.

GLOSSARY

Abdomen The rear part of a spider's body.

Annulations Alternating dark and pale bands on the legs.

Araneomorph A typical, 'true' spider, with jaws that close together (compare Mygalomorph).

Arthropod An animal with many-jointed legs and a skeleton (exoskeleton) on the outside of the body, as in crabs, insects and spiders.

Book lung Respiratory organ composed of a cavity containing layers through which the blood flows to absorb oxygen. Book lungs appear as pale squares on the underside of the abdomen. Primitive spiders have two pairs and true spiders usually have one pair (plus a system of tracheae).

Brood chamber A silk sac in which the female spider produces her young.

Carapace The shell-like covering over the first part of a spider's body (the cephalothorax).

Cardiac mark An elongate, diamond-shaped mark on the front of the abdomen (above the heart).

Cephalothorax The front part of the spider's body, i.e. the part which carries the legs.

Chelicerae The jaws of a spider. The base segment of each of the two chelicera supports a movable fang.

Chevrons Decorative marks (half diamonds) on the abdomen.

Cosmopolitan Occurring in many countries around the world.

Cribellum An organ which spins silk of an extremely fine and woolly quality. The cribellum lies just ahead of the spinnerets in a group of spiders known as the cribellates (lace-web weavers).

Cytotoxic A type of venom which causes damage to the body tissues.

Detritus Waste or decaying material on the ground.

Dragline The line of silk on which a spider drops down and then climbs back up.

Epigyne Surface features of the female's reproductive system.

Exuvium The old skin (exoskeleton) cast during moulting.

Gossamer Long, airborne lines of spider silk.

Hub The central circle of an orb-web.

Incubation Period of development for the eggs.

Kleptoparasite An animal that steals the food of another, e.g. a spider that feeds in the web of another species.

Liphistiomorph A spider belonging to the primitive suborder Liphistiomorphae.

Morphological Relating to the external appearance of an animal.

Mygalomorph A spider belonging to the suborder Mygalomorphae. These mostly large spiders, with jaws which strike downwards in parallel, are considered to be relatively primitive (see Araneomorph).

Neurotoxic A type of venom affecting the nervous system.

Pedipalps or palps Short, leg-like feelers either side of the mouthparts. In the adult male, the palps carry a pair of reproductive organs.

Pantropical Occurring throughout the tropical regions of the world.

Pedicel The narrow stalk connecting the cephalothorax and abdomen.

Radial thread One of a number of silk lines radiating out from the hub of an orb-web, like the spokes of a wheel.

Retreat A spider's shelter, usually made of silk.

Rhomboidal Diamond-shaped.

Sac (egg sac) A package of silk enclosing the eggs.

Signal line or **signal thread** A silk line connecting the spider with the web's hub.

Spinnerets Appendages at the end of the abdomen through which fine strands of silk emerge.

Spiral thread The thread that circles from the hub to the margin of the web.

Spur(s) Thorn-like projections on the legs and palps.

Stabilimentum A band of white silk usually in the form of a zigzag near the hub of the web. A stabilimentum is characteristic of spiders belonging to the genus *Argiope*.

Striae Lines on the surface of the body, especially lines radiating from a point.

Substrate The underlying ground, or a supporting structure.

Swathing band A thick band of silk used to wrap prey struggling in a web.

Tarantula One of the giant hairy spiders belonging to the family Theraphosidae. The term 'bird-eating' spider has the same meaning.

Tracheae Fine tubes which allow air from the respiratory openings to reach the body tissues.

Trip-line or **trip-thread** Silk lines extending from the opening of a spider's burrow. The lines communicate vibrations from passing insects to the waiting spider.

Tubercle(s) Thorn- or wart-like irregularities on the surface of the body.

INDEX